THE ULTIMATE ADULTING GUIDE

Learn to Manage Your Finances, Write Great Resumes, Simplify Meals, and Build Communication Skills and a Cozy Place.

JANINE DESIMONE

CONTENTS

Introduction	7
1. Moving Out and Independent Living	11
2. Culinary Skills and Home Management	21
3. Professional Development and Career Success	39
4. Financial Foundations for Young Adults	55
5. Health and Wellbeing Mastery	67
6. Relationship Management and Communication Skills	81
7. Social Etiquette and Cultural Competence	93
8. Digital Literacy and Online Safety	103
9. Personal Safety and Preparedness	113
10. Personal Growth and Life Planning	123
Conclusion	137
References	141

"The journey of a thousand miles begins with one step."

— LAO TZU

INTRODUCTION

You're standing in line at the grocery store, juggling a basket full of items you hope will last the week. You're trying to remember if you've paid the electricity bill. Meanwhile, your phone buzzes with a reminder for tomorrow's job interview. At that moment, you realize that adulting is not as simple as it seems. If you've ever found yourself in a similar situation, you're not alone. Transitioning into adulthood is a journey filled with unexpected turns and challenges.

The purpose of this book, "The Ultimate Adulting Guide: The Young Adults Handbook for Success." is to offer you the tools and insights needed to navigate this journey effectively. It's about equipping you with life skills that aren't taught in school but are vital for thriving in the real world. From understanding healthcare to managing your finances, this book guides you to make informed decisions and build a foundation for success.

This book covers a wide range of crucial topics for adult life. We'll dive into financial literacy, exploring budgeting, credit, and investing. We'll discuss health and wellbeing, including choosing the right insurance and maintaining a balanced lifestyle. Professional development will be a key focus, with tips on crafting a resume, acing interviews, and understanding workplace etiquette. Personal growth topics like mindfulness, setting boundaries, and effective communication will also be addressed, helping you to cultivate fulfilling relationships.

What sets this book apart from other guides is its practicality and positivity. You won't just find generic advice here. Each chapter is packed with actionable tips and real-life examples that you can relate to. This practical approach will equip you with the tools you need to confidently face the challenges of adulthood. Every chapter begins or ends with a quote designed to inspire and motivate you, reinforcing the belief that you have what it takes to succeed.

As a young adult, you face unique challenges and aspirations. This book speaks to you directly, acknowledging the obstacles you encounter and the dreams you hold. Whether stepping into your first job, moving into your own place, or figuring out how to balance a checkbook, this book is designed to meet you where you are and guide you toward where you want to be.

Let me introduce myself. I'm passionate about helping young adults like you navigate this complex phase of life. Having spent years observing the hurdles faced by individuals transitioning into adulthood, I felt compelled to compile this resource. My background in coaching and my own experiences, which I share throughout the book, have equipped me with insights that I'm eager to share. I aim to make your journey smoother and more rewarding, and to let you know that you're not alone in this.

As you turn the pages, expect to gain more than just knowledge. You'll learn to organize your life more effectively, face challenges confidently, and embrace growth opportunities. This book is not just a guide, but a companion, offering guidance and encouragement along the way. Engage with the content, take notes, and apply the lessons. The more actively you participate, the more you'll benefit.

Let's begin this journey with enthusiasm and determination. You can thrive in adulthood, and this book is here to help you do just that. Remember, every step you take brings you closer to becoming the person you aspire to be. As you embark on this adventure, remember this quote: "The future belongs to those who believe in the beauty of their dreams." You have the potential to create a fulfilling and successful life. Let's make it happen together.

CHAPTER 1

MOVING OUT AND INDEPENDENT LIVING

"Independence is the key to a strong and happy life."

— LAILAH GIFTY AKITA

Deciding to move out is not just about packing boxes and saying goodbye to your childhood room. It's a big step into independence, filled with excitement and a bit of anxiety. You might find yourself standing in an apartment with a view that's just about perfect, only to realize it's miles away from the nearest grocery store or public transport. Or maybe you find the ideal spot, only to discover that your dream apartment is way out of your budget. These scenarios are all too familiar for many young adults taking their first steps into independent living. This chapter will guide you through making informed decisions about where to live, ensuring you find a place that suits your needs and future aspirations. It will also provide crucial insights into understanding lease agreements, empowering you to navigate the legalities of renting effectively and with confidence.

1.1 ASSESSING WHERE TO LIVE: CHOOSING THE RIGHT LOCATION

Choosing where to live involves more than just picking a spot on a map. It requires careful consideration of various factors that can affect your daily life and long-term happiness. Proximity to your work or school is crucial. A short commute can save you valuable time and reduce stress while living too far away can make your daily routine more challenging. Access to public transportation is another vital consideration. Reliable transit can offer flexibility and cost savings, especially if you don't own a car. When evaluating potential areas, dig deeper by researching online neighborhood reviews. Websites like U.S. News offer insights into the cost of living, job market, and healthcare quality, helping you make an informed decision. Visiting neighborhoods at different times of the day can also provide a more complete picture of what living there might be like. It's surprising how a seemingly quiet street can transform at night or during rush hour.

Safety and amenities are vital components when assessing a location. Crime rates should be scrutinized, but remember that they don't always tell the whole story. Talking to residents and checking neighborhood watch programs can give a more nuanced perspective on safety. Amenities such as grocery stores, parks, and healthcare facilities contribute significantly to your quality of life. Having these nearby can make your life much more convenient, reducing the need for long trips to get essentials. Consider what is available now and what might be developed in the future. If you settle long-term, this foresight can enhance your living experience and increase property values.

Thinking ahead is essential when choosing a location. Consider your career trajectory and whether the area offers opportunities for growth or job changes. Living in a place with a booming job market can open doors for advancement and provide a safety net if your current job changes. If you plan to start a family, consider the quality of local schools and family-friendly amenities. These factors might not seem immediately relevant, especially if you're starting out. Still, they can become increasingly important as your life evolves. Balancing your present needs with future possibilities ensures that your choice of location supports your life now and adapts as your circumstances change.

Reflection Section: Evaluating Your Priorities

Take a moment to jot down your top three priorities when choosing a place to live. Consider what factors are most important for your lifestyle and future goals. Is it being close to work, having access to public transportation, or living in a neighborhood with many amenities? Reflecting on these priorities can help guide your decision-making and ensure your new home meets your needs.

1.2 TIPS FOR CHOOSING A ROOMMATE AND LIVING HARMONIOUSLY

Choosing a roommate is a bit like dating. You're looking for someone whose lifestyle aligns with yours, someone you can trust, and perhaps even someone you can call a friend. Imagine sharing a small apartment with someone whose idea of cleanliness radically differs from yours. You're meticulous, organizing your space with the precision of an interior designer. At the same time, your roommate sees laundry as an abstract art form scattered across every available surface. These differences can lead to tension and frustration if not addressed early. Evaluating potential roommates based on lifestyle habits and cleanliness standards is essential to avoid such scenarios. Are they early risers or night owls? Do they enjoy hosting parties every weekend, or do they prefer quiet nights in? Understanding these factors helps ensure you select someone who won't clash with your daily rhythm. Shared interests and schedules can also be vital. Suppose you both love binge-watching the same shows or share a passion for cooking. In that case, you'll likely find common ground that makes living together more enjoyable. This shared connection can bring a sense of optimism and hope to your roommate search, making the prospect of living with someone new more exciting.

Once you've found a potential roommate, setting clear expectations is crucial. This is where communication becomes your best friend. Sit down and have an open discussion about boundaries and responsibilities. It might feel awkward initially, but creating a roommate agreement can save a lot of headaches down the road. This agreement doesn't have to be a formal document. It's a mutual understanding of cleaning schedules, guest policies, and handling shared expenses. Establishing rules for shared spaces is equally important. Decide together how you'll manage areas like the kitchen and living room. Will you share groceries, or is each person responsible for their own? How will you handle cleaning these spaces? These discussions help prevent misunderstandings and foster a respectful living environment.

Maintaining a positive living environment requires ongoing effort and cooperation. Regularly scheduled house meetings can be an excellent way to check in and address issues before they escalate. These meetings are a chance to air grievances, celebrate victories, and plan for upcoming events. They don't have to be formal or lengthy. A quick chat over coffee can suffice. Keeping open lines of communication is vital for resolving issues promptly. Encourage each other to speak up if something bothers you, and listen actively when your roommate wants to talk. This openness helps build trust and ensures minor annoyances don't become more significant conflicts. This commitment to open communication will reassure you and your roommate, creating a secure and harmonious living environment where everyone's voice is heard and respected.

Even in the best situations, conflicts can arise. The key is handling disagreements constructively. When it comes to dividing chores, fairness is essential. Consider creating a chore wheel or calendar that rotates responsibilities. This system ensures that duties are shared equally and that no one feels overburdened. Managing noise levels and privacy is another common challenge. Discuss your preferences for quiet time and how you'll signal when you need space. Agreeing on quiet hours, especially evenings, can help prevent disruptions and maintain a peaceful home environment. Other potential conflicts include differing opinions on guests, handling of shared items, or even personal habits. It's essential to address these issues openly and respectfully, always keeping in mind the goal of maintaining a harmonious living environment.

Case Study: Roommate Harmony Checklist

To help you navigate this process, consider creating a "Roommate Harmony Checklist." This tool can guide your initial discussions and be a reference point throughout your cohabitation. Include categories like cleaning preferences, guest policies, and financial responsibilities. Regularly review and update this checklist as needed to ensure it continues to reflect your living arrangement. This proactive approach can enhance your living experience, fostering a harmonious and enjoyable home life.

Choosing a roommate involves thoughtful consideration and clear communication. By assessing compatibility, setting expectations, and maintaining open dialogue, you can create a living environment that is functional but also supportive and fulfilling. While the process requires effort, the result—a harmonious home—makes every conversation and compromise worthwhile.

1.3 UNDERSTANDING RENTAL AGREEMENTS AND TENANT RIGHTS

Stepping into the world of renting can feel like navigating a maze of unfamiliar terms and legal jargon. It's easy to feel overwhelmed when you're handed a rental agreement, a hefty document that holds the key to your future home. However, understanding this agreement is crucial, as it outlines your rights and obligations as a tenant. At its core, a rental agreement includes several key components you must comprehend. The lease duration, for instance, specifies how long you're committing to stay, whether it's a year-long lease or a month-to-month arrangement. Renewal options are equally important in determining what happens when your lease term expires. Knowing whether you can renew under the same terms or if there will be renegotiations can save you from unexpected surprises. Rent payment terms are another fundamental aspect. This section details when your rent is due, acceptable payment methods, and penalties for late payments. It's essential to be clear on these terms to avoid falling afoul of your landlord and incurring unnecessary fees. If you're a pet owner, pay special attention to the pet policy. Some agreements require additional deposits or specific insurance if you're bringing a furry friend along. Understanding these stipulations can help avoid conflicts and ensure a smooth move-in process.

Tenant rights are another critical area to understand. You have the right to a habitable living space, which means your rental should meet basic safety and health standards. If issues like broken heating or pest infestations arise, your landlord must address them promptly. Familiarize yourself with the procedures for addressing maintenance issues. Know how to report problems and the expected timeline for repairs. This knowledge empowers you to advocate for yourself and ensures your living conditions remain comfortable and safe. Many renters overlook the importance of knowing their rights, which can lead to exploitation. By staying informed, you protect yourself from unfair treatment and ensure your landlord upholds their agreement.

Negotiating lease terms might seem daunting, especially if it's your first time renting. However, it's an opportunity to tailor the agreement to better suit your needs. For instance, don't hesitate to request repairs or improvements before signing if the apartment needs upgrades. This might include updating appliances, fixing leaks, or addressing safety concerns. Some landlords might be open to negotiating rent increases, especially if you're a long-term tenant or renewing your lease. You can also negotiate deposit terms by asking for a portion to be used as advance rent. Approaching these discussions confidently and clearly can lead to a more favorable living arrangement without the pressure of unmanageable costs.

Document everything when you move into a new place. This might seem tedious, but thorough documentation is your best defense against future disputes. Start by photographing the property's condition before you move in. Capture any existing damage, from minor scratches to more significant issues like broken fixtures or stained carpets. These photos indicate that you didn't cause the damage, protecting your security deposit when it's time to move out. Keep copies of all correspondence with your landlord, including emails, texts, and written notices. This paper trail is invaluable if disagreements arise, as it clearly records what was communicated and agreed upon. Whether confirming a repair request or discussing lease renewals, documentation ensures clarity and accountability on both sides.

Leasing an apartment is more than just signing on the dotted line; it's about establishing a secure and agreeable living situation. With a clear understanding of the rental agreement and your rights as a tenant, you can confidently move forward, knowing you're well-prepared for the responsibilities and challenges that may arise. As you settle into your new home, remember that knowledge and preparation are your allies in this exciting chapter of your life.

1.4 SECURING RENTAL INSURANCE AND PROTECTING YOUR BELONGINGS

Stepping into your new rental apartment, you may not immediately consider what happens if something goes wrong. Yet, safeguarding your personal belongings and financial wellbeing with rental insurance is a prudent step. Rental insurance serves as a safety net, covering your possessions against unforeseen events like theft or damage. Imagine returning home to find your laptop missing, the one you rely on for work and stream your favorite shows. With rental insurance, you have the assurance that your stolen items can be replaced, alleviating the stress of financial loss. Beyond protecting personal property, rental insurance often includes liability coverage. If someone gets injured in your home —perhaps tripping over that rug you've meant to fix—your policy can cover the legal expenses. This dual protection makes rental insurance a crucial component of your new independent lifestyle.

Selecting the right rental insurance policy might seem daunting, but it's all about understanding your needs and comparing options. Start by assessing the coverage limits and deductibles of policies. Coverage limits refer to the maximum amount the insurer will pay for a covered loss, while the deductible is what you pay out-of-pocket before insurance kicks in. Choosing a policy with appropriate limits for your possessions is key. You don't want to overpay for coverage you don't need, but you also want to avoid being underinsured. Compare policy premiums from different providers, considering both cost and coverage. Some insurers offer lower premiums but with higher deductibles or less comprehensive coverage. Balancing these factors will help you find a policy that suits your financial situation and peace of mind.

Once you've chosen a policy, it's time to inventory and value your belongings. This step might sound tedious, but it's essential for ensuring adequate coverage. Begin by creating a detailed inventory list of your possessions. Document everything from electronics to furniture, noting the brand, model, and purchase price. This information provides a clear picture of what you own and its value. Using apps to store receipts and photos can simplify this process. Apps like Sortly or Home Inventory allow you to upload images and documents, creating a virtual record of your items. This digital archive can be invaluable if you need to file a claim, as it provides proof of ownership and value, streamlining the reimbursement process.

Understanding policy exclusions is another critical aspect of rental insurance. While policies cover many scenarios, they often exclude certain events. Flood and earthquake exclusions are standard, meaning you may need additional coverage if you live in an area prone to these natural disasters. High-value items, like jewelry or art, also have limitations. Insurers often cap the payout on such items unless you purchase additional riders or endorsements. Awareness of these exclusions ensures you're not caught off guard when you need to make a claim. Discuss these aspects with your insurance provider to tailor your policy to your needs, ensuring comprehensive protection.

Imagine your apartment as a castle, with rental insurance acting as the moat, keeping potential threats at bay. Securing the right policy protects your belongings, financial stability, and peace of mind. This proactive step lets you focus on the joys of independent living, knowing you're prepared for the unexpected. As you settle into your new place, take a moment to appreciate the security you've built, not just with walls and locks but with the knowledge and protection of rental insurance.

CHAPTER 2

CULINARY SKILLS AND HOME MANAGEMENT

"A house is made of walls and beams; a home is built with love and dreams."

— RALPH WALDO EMERSON

Picture this: you're staring into your fridge, wondering what you can whip up with a half-empty jar of salsa, some wilted spinach, and a leftover grilled chicken. The prospect of adulting often includes these moments of culinary confusion. Yet, mastering your kitchen doesn't have to feel like a daunting task. You can transform this chaos into culinary competence with some foresight and creativity. This chapter is your guide to navigating the kitchen with confidence and flair. By embracing meal prep, you'll streamline your cooking routine and save time and money while nourishing your body with wholesome, homemade meals.

2:1 EASY AND BUDGET-FRIENDLY MEAL PREP

Meal prep is a game-changer when it comes to saving both time and money. By planning your meals in advance and preparing them in bulk, you can significantly reduce the stress of daily cooking. Imagine having a week's worth of delicious meals ready to go, freeing up your evenings for relaxation or socializing. Batch cooking, which involves preparing large quantities of a dish, such as a hearty chili or a flavorful curry, and freezing individual portions, is a key strategy here. This approach not only ensures nutritious meals but also allows you to take advantage of sales and discounts on bulk ingredients. Planning meals around what's on sale can lead to substantial savings, transforming shopping from a dreaded chore into a strategic opportunity to cut costs. I'll delve into the benefits of batch cooking in more detail in the next section.

When it comes to meal prep, simplicity is your ally. Opt for recipes that are not only nutritious but also cater to diverse dietary preferences. One-pot meals are a fantastic starting point. Think of dishes like a vibrant vegetable stir-fry or a comforting chicken and rice casserole. These meals are easy to prepare and minimize cleanup—a win-win for anyone leading a busy life. For those following vegetarian or vegan diets, consider options like a hearty lentil soup or a protein-packed quinoa salad. These budget-friendly dishes offer a wide array of nutrients, ensuring your body gets nourishment without breaking the bank. If you have specific dietary preferences or restrictions, such as gluten-free or dairy-free, you can quickly adapt these recipes to suit your needs. For instance, you can use gluten-free pasta in a one-pot dish or substitute dairy with plant-based alternatives in a casserole. This flexibility allows you to enjoy delicious meals that align with your dietary requirements. I'll provide some specific tips on how to make these adaptations in the next section.

Establish a routine that works for you to make meal prep as efficient as possible. Start by creating a weekly menu that outlines what you'll eat each day. This step helps organize your shopping list and reduces food waste, as you'll buy only what you need. I'll provide some tips on how to create a balanced and varied weekly menu in the next section. Once your plan is set, dedicate time to prep ingredients. Efficient chopping and portioning techniques can save you time and ensure meal consistency. Consider investing in quality storage containers that can transition from freezer to microwave, making reheating a breeze. By dedicating a few hours each week to meal prep, you'll set yourself up for success and minimize the temptation of takeout.

While meal prep offers many benefits, it's not without its challenges. Preventing food waste is a common concern, especially when ingredients spoil before you can use them. To combat this, be realistic about portion sizes and plan meals with similar ingredients, ensuring nothing goes to waste. Keeping meals fresh throughout the week requires proper storage techniques. Use airtight containers to maintain flavor and freshness, and consider labeling each meal with the preparation date to track its shelf life. If you are bored with repetitive meals, switch spices and sauces to keep things interesting.

Reflection Section: Meal Prep Success Checklist

Reflect on your meal prep journey by creating a "Meal Prep Success Checklist." Include steps like planning your weekly menu, batch cooking, and utilizing proper storage techniques. Regularly review this checklist to identify areas for improvement and celebrate your progress. This proactive approach can enhance your meal prep experience, ensuring it remains a valuable tool in your adulting arsenal.

By incorporating these strategies into your routine, meal prep becomes less of a chore and more of a rewarding habit. You will gain control over your diet and expenses and cultivate a sense of accomplishment as you master the art of efficient, budget-friendly cooking. This sense of accomplishment will make you feel proud and satisfied with your progress in adulting.

SAMPLE MEALS

1. One-Pot Veggie Stir-Fry

Ingredients:

- 2 cups mixed vegetables (fresh or frozen)
- 1 cup cooked brown rice or quinoa
- 1 tbsp olive oil
- 2 tbsp soy sauce (or tamari for gluten-free)
- 1 tsp sesame oil (optional)
- 1 tbsp sesame seeds (optional)
- 1 clove garlic, minced
- 1/2 tsp ground ginger or fresh ginger
- 1/4 cup green onions, chopped

Instructions:

1. Heat olive oil in a large pan or wok over medium heat. Add garlic and ginger, and sauté for 1 minute.
2. Add the mixed vegetables and cook for 5-7 minutes until tender.
3. Add cooked rice or quinoa, soy sauce, and sesame oil. Stir everything together.
4. Cook for another 3-5 minutes until everything is heated through.
5. Top with sesame seeds and green onions for extra flavor.

Tips: This dish is great for meal prep because you can make a large batch and store it in airtight containers for the week. You can also add tofu, chicken, or shrimp for extra protein.

2. *Chicken and Rice Casserole*

Ingredients:

- 2 chicken breasts, cooked and shredded
- 2 cups cooked rice (white or brown)
- 1 can of cream of mushroom soup (or make your own with vegetable broth)
- 1 cup frozen peas or mixed veggies
- 1/2 cup shredded cheese (optional for non-dairy, use dairy-free cheese)
- Salt and pepper to taste
- 1/2 tsp garlic powder
- 1/2 tsp onion powder
- 1 tbsp olive oil or butter

Instructions:

1. Preheat oven to 375°F (190°C).
2. In a large mixing bowl, combine cooked rice, shredded chicken, peas, soup, and spices.
3. Spread mixture into a greased casserole dish and top with cheese (if using).
4. Cover with foil and bake for 25 minutes. Remove foil and bake for another 10 minutes to allow cheese to melt.
5. Serve in individual portions and store leftovers in airtight containers.

Tips: This recipe is a great one for meal prep because it can be frozen in portions for later use. You can also swap out chicken for ground turkey, beef, or even beans for a vegetarian option.

3. Hearty Lentil Soup

Ingredients:

- 1 cup dried lentils (green or brown), rinsed
- 1 can diced tomatoes
- 1 large carrot, chopped
- 2 celery stalks, chopped
- 1 onion, chopped
- 2 cloves garlic, minced
- 1 tsp cumin
- 1 tsp paprika
- 4 cups vegetable broth or water
- Salt and pepper to taste
- 1 tbsp olive oil

Instructions:

1. In a large pot, heat olive oil over medium heat. Add garlic, onion, carrot, and celery, and sauté for 5 minutes.
2. Add lentils, diced tomatoes, spices, and broth. Bring to a boil, then reduce heat and let simmer for 30-40 minutes, or until lentils are tender.
3. Season with salt and pepper to taste.
4. Store in individual portions for easy lunches or dinners throughout the week.

Tips: Lentil soup is perfect for meal prep and can be easily frozen. Add some greens (spinach or kale) in the last 10 minutes of cooking for added nutrition.

4. Quinoa Salad with Chickpeas and Veggies

Ingredients:

- 1 cup cooked quinoa (or bulgur wheat)
- 1 can chickpeas, drained and rinsed
- 1 cucumber, diced
- 1 bell pepper, diced
- 1/4 cup red onion, diced
- 1/4 cup olive oil
- 2 tbsp lemon juice
- 1 tbsp Dijon mustard
- Salt and pepper to taste

Instructions:

1. In a large bowl, combine the cooked quinoa, chickpeas, cucumber, bell pepper, and red onion.
2. In a small bowl, whisk together olive oil, lemon juice, Dijon mustard, salt, and pepper to create a dressing.
3. Pour dressing over the salad and toss to coat evenly.
4. Chill in the fridge for at least 30 minutes before serving.

Tips: This salad is perfect for meal prep as it stores well for several days in the fridge. It can be eaten as a light lunch or dinner, and you can add additional protein like grilled chicken or feta cheese if desired.

5. Easy Veggie Frittata

Ingredients:

- 8 large eggs
- 1/2 cup milk (dairy or plant-based)
- 1 cup spinach, chopped
- 1/2 cup bell peppers, diced
- 1/2 cup mushrooms, sliced
- 1/2 cup shredded cheese (optional for non-dairy, use dairy-free cheese)
- Salt and pepper to taste
- 1 tbsp olive oil

Instructions:

1. Preheat oven to 375°F (190°C).
2. In an oven-safe skillet, heat olive oil over medium heat. Add bell peppers, mushrooms, and spinach, and cook until soft (5 minutes).
3. In a bowl, whisk together eggs, milk, salt, and pepper.
4. Pour egg mixture over the cooked vegetables in the skillet, then sprinkle with cheese (if using).
5. Transfer skillet to the oven and bake for 15-20 minutes, or until eggs are set and slightly golden on top.
6. Slice and serve. This frittata can be stored in the fridge for a few days and is great for breakfast or a light dinner.

Tips: Frittatas are incredibly versatile—add any leftover vegetables or meats for an easy, customizable meal. They also freeze well if you need to prepare ahead for busy weeks.

Meal Prep Tips for Success:

- **Batch cook:** Prepare large portions of these meals and store them in individual containers. This will save time during the week and reduce the temptation of takeout.
- **Use leftovers creatively:** Use leftover quinoa salad as a filling for wraps, or turn leftover veggie stir-fry into a lunch bowl with a fresh protein.
- **Adapt meals to your needs:** All these recipes are customizable. You can easily swap out ingredients based on what you have on hand or specific dietary needs.

2:2 GROCERY SHOPPING AND FOOD SAFETY TIPS

Walking into a grocery store without a plan can feel like stepping into a maze, where every aisle has the potential to lead you astray with enticing deals and colorful displays. But with a comprehensive shopping list in hand, crafted after taking inventory of what you already have at home, you're in control. This simple act of planning can help you avoid impulse purchases, keep your spending in check, and ensure you don't forget any critical ingredients for your planned meals. This sense of organization and control will make your grocery shopping and meal prep more efficient and less stressful.

Selecting fresh and quality ingredients is crucial for both taste and nutrition. Start with the produce section, where choosing ripe fruits and vegetables can be an art form. Look for vibrant colors and firm textures, which typically indicate freshness. Give fruits like avocados a gentle squeeze—if they yield slightly, they're ripe and ready to eat. Vegetables should be crisp and free from blemishes. When selecting meat, consider the color and smell; fresh beef should have a bright hue and a neutral odor. Checking expiration dates on packaged goods is vital. Always reach for the items at the back of the shelf as they usually have a longer shelf life, thanks to the store's rotation practices.

Food safety is paramount in preventing illness and ensuring your meals are as healthy as they are delicious. Proper storage is your first line of defense. Organize your refrigerator by placing raw meats on the bottom shelf to prevent their juices from contaminating other foods. Store perishable items like dairy and eggs in the main compartment where the temperature is most stable. Freezing can extend the life of meats and leftovers; use airtight containers to prevent freezer burn. Airtight containers create a barrier against air and moisture, which can cause freezer burn and spoilage. When using airtight containers, leave some space at the top to allow for expansion during freezing. Separating raw and cooked foods is another fundamental rule. Use different cutting boards for meats and vegetables, and always wash your hands and utensils thoroughly after handling raw items to prevent cross-contamination. These practices will give you the confidence and security to enjoy your cooking without worry.

Reducing grocery costs doesn't mean compromising on quality. Consider buying in bulk for non-perishable items like grains and pasta, as this often results in lower unit prices and fewer trips to the store. Local farmers' markets are treasure troves for fresh, affordable produce. Shopping seasonally at these markets supports local farmers and offers fresher options at potentially lower prices. Keep an eye out for deals and discounts, and don't shy away from store-brand products—they often provide the same quality as name-brand ones at a fraction of the price. Implementing these strategies allows you to enjoy nutritious meals without stretching your budget.

Interactive Element: Grocery Savvy Challenge

Challenge yourself to a "Grocery Savvy Challenge" next time you shop. Aim to stick strictly to your list, compare unit prices, and choose at least one seasonal or local item. Record your total savings and reflect on the quality of your purchases. This exercise sharpens your shopping skills and enhances your awareness of spending habits and product quality.

2.3 ESSENTIAL KITCHEN TOOLS AND HOW TO USE THEM

Stepping into a kitchen without the right tools is like trying to write a novel without a pen. To embark on your culinary adventures, you need a few essential items that will make cooking not just possible but enjoyable. A chef's knife tops the list—think of it as your trusty sidekick. This tool is indispensable for nearly every task, from slicing vegetables to dicing meats. Pair it with a sturdy cutting board, preferably hardwood or thick bamboo, to provide a stable surface that keeps your knife sharp and your fingers safe. Next, invest in a non-stick skillet, perfect for everything from frying eggs to searing chicken. Its smooth surface ensures easy cleanup and healthier cooking with less oil. Complement this with a saucepan, ideal for simmering sauces or boiling pasta. Together, these tools form the backbone of your kitchen arsenal, enabling you to efficiently tackle a wide range of recipes.

Selecting quality kitchen tools doesn't mean you have to empty your wallet. Focus on durability and material when choosing your equipment. Stainless steel and cast iron are excellent choices for longevity and heat distribution. Stainless steel is versatile and rust-resistant, making it suitable for various cooking methods. Cast iron, while heavier, provides even heat and can go from stovetop to oven seamlessly. When purchasing knives, look for full-tang options where the blade extends through the handle, offering better balance and strength. You don't need the priciest brand to achieve great results—many affordable options provide excellent performance, exceptionally when cared for properly. Prioritize quality over quantity; a few well-chosen tools will better serve you than a drawer full of gadgets that gather dust.

Proper care and maintenance can significantly extend the life of your kitchen tools, ensuring they serve you well for years. Start with your chef's knife, which should be sharpened regularly to maintain its edge. A dull knife is ineffective and dangerous, as it requires more force and can slip easily. Use a sharpening stone or a honing rod, and learn the proper technique to keep your knife in top condition. For your non-stick skillet, avoid using metal utensils that can scratch and degrade the coating. Instead, opt for wooden or silicone tools. When cleaning, use warm, soapy water and a soft sponge; harsh scrubbers can damage the surface. Remember to rinse with water for cast iron skillets, dry thoroughly, and apply a thin layer of oil to prevent rusting. Regular maintenance preserves your tools and enhances their performance, making cooking more enjoyable.

Organizing your kitchen tools efficiently can transform your cooking space into a functional haven. Drawer organizers are a simple yet effective way to keep utensils in order, ensuring you can find what you need without rummaging through clutter. Invest in a magnetic strip or wall-mounted rack to store knives safely and accessibly, freeing up valuable counter space. For pots and pans, consider installing hooks or shelves that allow you to hang them within easy reach. This setup makes the most of vertical space and keeps your kitchen tidy and professional. Group similar items, such as baking tools or measuring cups, to streamline your cooking process. A well-organized kitchen is not just about aesthetics; it enhances efficiency, allowing you to focus on the joy of creating delicious meals.

2:4 MASTERING LAUNDRY AND ORGANIZING YOUR SPACE

Laundry day might seem mundane, but it's crucial for maintaining your wardrobe and confidence. Start by sorting your laundry into piles based on color and fabric type. This simple step prevents colors from bleeding and helps keep fabric quality. Whites, darks, and colors should each have their own pile. Delicate fabrics like silk or cashmere require special attention; use a gentle cycle and cold water to preserve their integrity. Understanding your washing machine settings can make a world of difference. Most machines offer cycles for different fabric types, and using the right one can extend the life of your clothes. If you're dealing with stubborn stains, pre-treat them before washing them. Dab a stain remover on the spot and let it sit for a few minutes. This proactive approach increases the chances of removing the stain without damaging the fabric.

A well-organized living space is more than just visually appealing. It can significantly enhance your efficiency and overall quality of life. Begin by decluttering your home—set aside time to go through your belongings and decide what to keep, donate, or discard. The goal is to create a space that feels open and manageable. Utilize storage solutions like bins and shelves to keep items organized and accessible. Labeling boxes can help you locate things quickly, saving time and reducing frustration. Consider investing in storage furniture, such as ottomans with hidden compartments or shelving units that double as room dividers. These pieces provide storage and add to your space's aesthetic, creating a harmonious balance between form and function.

The state of your living environment can profoundly impact your mental wellbeing. A tidy home can reduce stress and foster a sense of calm, allowing you to focus on what truly matters. Clutter can be overwhelming, constantly reminding of tasks left undone. By organizing your space, you create a sanctuary to recharge and relax. A clean home is also healthy, free from dust and allergens that can impact your health. This clarity and order allow you to approach each day with a fresh perspective, enhancing productivity and mood.

Living in a small space doesn't mean sacrificing comfort or style. Maximize your living area by choosing multi-functional furniture. A sofa bed, for instance, can serve as a couch by day and a bed by night, perfect for small apartments or studios. Vertical storage solutions are another effective way to maximize limited space. Wall-mounted shelves or tall bookcases draw the eye upward, creating the illusion of height and offering additional storage without taking up valuable floor space. Consider using under-bed storage bins or hanging organizers for those with limited closet space. These options keep your belongings neatly stored yet easily accessible, transforming your small living area into a well-organized retreat.

2:5 BASIC HOME MAINTENANCE AND DIY REPAIRS

Owning or renting a place means that, sooner or later, you'll face the inevitable: things break, wear out, or need a little TLC. Regular home maintenance is crucial to avoiding more significant headaches down the road. It might not be glamorous, but cleaning gutters is a task that can save you from water damage or even mold. Clogged gutters cause water to overflow, potentially damaging your home's foundation. Clearing leaves and debris, especially during autumn, ensures proper drainage. Similarly, checking for leaks and drafts is an often-overlooked maintenance task that can improve comfort and reduce energy bills. Drafts sneak in through windows and doors, letting your precious heating or air conditioning escape. Simple fixes like weather stripping or caulking can make a significant difference in keeping your home cozy and efficient.

A little know-how can go a long way when fixing common household problems. Take unclogging a sink, for example. It's a straightforward task that doesn't require a plumber. Often, a plunger or a simple mixture of baking soda and vinegar can do the trick, breaking down the gunk that's built up over time. Hanging pictures might seem trivial, but doing it correctly prevents unnecessary holes in your walls and ensures your artwork stays put. Use a level and the correct hardware for your wall type—drywall or plaster—to get it right the first time. Patching small holes in walls is another skill worth having. A bit of spackling paste and a putty knife can turn unsightly blemishes into smooth surfaces, ready for a fresh coat of paint.

Every home should have an essential toolkit for minor repairs. Start with a reliable hammer and screwdriver set, indispensable for countless tasks. Whether assembling furniture or fixing a loose hinge, these tools are your go-to. An adjustable wrench is another essential item, perfect for tightening bolts or working on plumbing fixtures. Look for tools that feel comfortable in your hand and offer a good grip; they don't have to be expensive, just durable. A tape measure is also helpful for everything from hanging curtains to planning new furniture layouts. With these tools, you're prepared to tackle most minor issues without delay, saving time and money by avoiding unnecessary service calls.

Recognizing when to call in the professionals is as important as knowing when to DIY. Electrical issues, for example, should be handled with extreme caution. Suppose you're dealing with anything more complicated than changing a light bulb or replacing a battery. In that case, it's best to consult an electrician. Faulty wiring can pose serious risks, including fire hazards. Similarly, persistent plumbing problems like recurring clogs or leaks can escalate quickly. A professional plumber can diagnose and fix issues you might not be equipped to handle, preventing further damage and higher costs in the future. Knowing your limits is crucial to maintaining safety and ensuring the job is done right.

You'll discover a sense of empowerment and independence as you become more proficient in maintaining and repairing your home. These skills save money and provide the satisfaction of knowing you can handle what life throws at you. Whether fixing a leaky faucet or ensuring your space remains inviting and comfortable, being proactive about home maintenance pays off in the long run. You'll find that a well-kept home is not just a place to live but a reflection of your ability to manage and improve your surroundings. With these fundamentals in place, you're ready to tackle the next aspects of adulting, seamlessly transitioning into the financial savvy that will further support your newfound independence.

CHAPTER 3

PROFESSIONAL DEVELOPMENT AND CAREER SUCCESS

"Opportunities don't happen, you create them."

— CHRIS GROSSER

Imagine standing at the threshold of your career, resume in hand, and staring at the job market like a vast ocean. Your resume is your vessel and needs to be strong enough to navigate the choppy waters of professional life. Crafting a resume that stands out is not just about listing your experiences; it's about telling your story in a way that resonates with potential employers. It's your first impression, and unlike a conversation, it doesn't have the benefit of body language or tone to back it up. Everything depends on how well you articulate your value on paper. As you embark on this endeavor, remember that your resume is a strategic document and should be treated as such.

3:1 CRAFTING A STANDOUT RESUME

To structure a resume for maximum impact, start with your contact information and a professional summary. Your contact section should be straightforward and unambiguous, including your full name, phone number, email address, and LinkedIn profile link, if applicable. Avoid using unprofessional email addresses; instead, opt for a simple combination of your name. The professional summary is your elevator pitch in written form. It's a concise paragraph highlighting who you are, what you bring to the table, and what you want to achieve in your career. Craft this section with care, as it sets the tone for the rest of your resume. Avoid generic statements and focus on what makes you unique and valuable as a candidate.

Diving deeper, your experience and skills sections are where you can truly shine. List your work experience in reverse chronological order, starting with your most recent position. For each role, include your job title, the company name, and the dates of employment. When describing your duties and achievements, use bullet points for clarity and focus on what you accomplished rather than just what you did. Action verbs like "implemented," "designed," or "managed" convey dynamism and initiative. Quantifying your achievements with metrics adds weight to your claims. For instance, "increased sales by 20%" is more impactful than "responsible for sales." This approach highlights your contributions and demonstrates your ability to drive results.

Tailoring your resume for specific job applications is crucial in the competitive job market. This means customizing it each time you apply for a new position. Start by carefully reading the job description and identifying keywords and phrases that align with your experience. These keywords are often the skills and attributes the employer is seeking. Integrating them naturally into your resume increases the likelihood that automated systems, frequently used by companies to screen applicants, will flag your application for further review. Additionally, highlight relevant experiences that mirror the job requirements. If a position requires project management skills and you've successfully led a team project, ensure that experience takes center stage.

While crafting your resume, focusing on clarity and conciseness is essential. Avoid the temptation to overload your resume with irrelevant information. Please keep it to one page, especially early in your career. Each word should serve a purpose, contributing to the narrative you want to present. Steer clear of industry jargon that might confuse rather than illuminate. Instead, use straightforward language that anyone can understand. Proofread meticulously to avoid typos and grammatical errors. Such mistakes can undermine your professionalism and attention to detail.

Interactive Element: Resume Revision Checklist

Create a "Resume Revision Checklist" to ensure you cover all bases. Include items like verifying contact information, refining your professional summary, incorporating action verbs, quantifying achievements, tailoring content to the job description, and proofreading for errors. Use this checklist when you tailor your resume to keep it polished and practical.

Sample Resume Outline:

1. Contact Information

- **Full Name**
- **Phone Number** (Use a professional voicemail greeting)
- **Email Address** (Use a professional email—ideally, a combination of your first and last name)
- **LinkedIn Profile** (Optional, but highly recommended)
- **Portfolio or Personal Website** (If applicable)

2. Professional Summary (Elevator Pitch)

- **Purpose:** A brief paragraph (3-4 sentences) that highlights:
  - Who you are professionally
  - What makes you stand out
  - Your key skills or experiences
  - What you're looking to achieve in your next role
- **Tips:**
  - Keep it concise and tailored to the position you're applying for
  - Focus on your strengths and unique qualifications
  - Avoid generic or overused phrases like "hardworking" or "team player"

3. Work Experience (Listed in Reverse Chronological Order)

- **Job Title**
- **Company Name**
- **Dates of Employment** (Month/Year format)

- **Job Description:** Use bullet points to describe key responsibilities and accomplishments. Focus on:
  - Action verbs (e.g., "managed," "designed," "increased")
  - Quantifiable achievements (e.g., "increased sales by 20%")
  - Specific contributions that made a positive impact
- **Example:**
  - **Marketing Coordinator**
  - XYZ Corporation — May 2020 – Present
    - Managed social media strategy, increasing engagement by 30%
    - Designed and launched a new product campaign, leading to a 15% increase in sales

4. Skills

- **Technical Skills** (e.g., Microsoft Office, Adobe Creative Suite, HTML, etc.)
- **Soft Skills** (e.g., Communication, Problem-Solving, Time Management)
- **Industry-Specific Skills** (Tailor this section to the job you're applying for)
- **Certifications or Training** (If applicable)

5. Education

- **Degree** (e.g., Bachelor's in Marketing)
- **University Name**
- **Graduation Year** (or expected year)
- **Relevant Coursework/Academic Achievements** (Optional, if early in your career)

6. Additional Sections (Optional, based on relevance)

- **Volunteer Experience** (If applicable)
  - Role/Organization
  - Dates
  - Key contributions
- **Awards & Honors**
- **Languages** (If applicable)
- **Projects** (If applicable, particularly for tech or creative roles)
  - Project name
  - Role/Contribution
  - Outcome/Impact

7. Tailoring the Resume for Specific Job Applications

- **Research the Job Description:** Highlight key skills, responsibilities, and qualifications from the job posting.
- **Include Relevant Keywords:** Identify keywords from the job description and integrate them naturally into your resume to increase your chances of passing through applicant tracking systems (ATS).
- **Showcase Relevant Experience:** Move the most relevant experiences to the top of your work history and highlight them in the job description.

8. Final Touches

- **Proofread for Typos and Errors:** Mistakes can diminish your credibility.
- **Limit to One Page (Early Career):** Especially for those early in their career, brevity is crucial.

- **Use a Clean, Professional Format:** Easy-to-read font (e.g., Arial, Calibri) and appropriate font size (10–12 pt).
- **Avoid Clutter:** Only include information that adds value to your narrative and showcases your qualifications.

Interactive Element: Resume Revision Checklist

- **Contact Info:** Is your phone number professional? Do you have a LinkedIn URL included?
- **Professional Summary:** Does it clearly state your value proposition? Is it tailored to the job you're applying for?
- **Work Experience:** Are your job titles and accomplishments clearly stated? Did you quantify your impact where possible?
- **Skills:** Are they relevant to the position? Have you tailored them to the job description?
- **Education:** Is your education section updated with your most recent achievements?
- **Proofreading:** Did you check for any typos, grammatical errors, or formatting issues?

Avoiding common pitfalls can significantly enhance your resume's effectiveness. Overloading it with irrelevant information can dilute your key messages, leaving recruiters unsure of your core competencies. Similarly, typos and grammatical errors can distract from your achievements. Remember, your resume reflects you—make it as precise and compelling as you are.

3.2 ACING THE JOB INTERVIEW WITH CONFIDENCE

Walking into a job interview can feel like stepping onto a stage with all eyes on you, eager to see what you bring to the table. It's a chance to showcase your skills and personality. Still, preparation is the key to ensuring your performance is memorable for all the right reasons. Start by researching the company culture. Dive into their website, explore their social media presence, and read up on any recent news articles or press releases. Understanding the company's values and ethos will give you a sense of what they're looking for in an employee and how you can align your responses to match their expectations. It's not just about having the right skills; it's about fitting into the team and contributing to the company's mission.

Furthermore, understanding the role and its requirements is crucial. Study the job description carefully, noting any specific responsibilities or skills mentioned. This knowledge will allow you to tailor your responses, demonstrating that you have the expertise they need.

As you prepare, remember that interviews often include a variety of questions, and being ready to tackle them confidently is key. Behavioral questions usually start with prompts like "Tell me about a time when…" These questions aim to gauge how you've handled situations in the past, providing insight into how you might perform in the future. Structure your responses using the STAR method—Situation, Task, Action, Result. This approach ensures clarity and focus, showing the interviewer that you can think logically and reflect on your experiences. Salary expectation questions can also be tricky. Research industry standards for the role and location beforehand to provide a realistic and informed range. Avoid discussing salary too early in the interview unless prompted. Instead, focus on conveying your enthusiasm for the role and the value you bring.

Interview nerves are natural, but they don't have to be overwhelming. Employing techniques to stay calm and focused can make a significant difference. Deep breathing exercises are simple yet effective. Before the interview, take a few moments to inhale deeply through your nose, hold, and exhale slowly through your mouth. This process helps calm your nerves and center your thoughts. Visualization is another powerful tool. Picture yourself succeeding in the interview—speaking clearly, smiling, and engaging positively with the interviewer. Such mental rehearsals can boost your confidence and reduce anxiety. Practicing with mock interviews is also invaluable. Ask a friend or mentor to simulate an interview, providing feedback on your responses and demeanor. This practice helps desensitize you to the interview environment, making the real thing feel less daunting.

After the interview, it's crucial to follow up professionally. Sending a thank-you note is a small gesture with a significant impact. In your note, express gratitude for the opportunity and reiterate your interest in the role. Mention something specific discussed during the interview to personalize your message and keep you fresh in the interviewer's mind. This simple act reflects professionalism and attention to detail.

Additionally, take time to evaluate your performance objectively. Reflect on what went well and where you could improve. This self-assessment is essential to personal growth and helps refine your skills for future interviews. Consider journaling your experiences and noting any patterns or recurring challenges. This record will serve as a valuable resource, guiding you toward more successful interviews in the future.

3.3 PROFESSIONAL ETIQUETTE AND WORKPLACE DYNAMICS

Professional etiquette is the set of unwritten rules that govern how we interact in the workplace. The framework supports a positive and productive environment where effective communication and mutual respect are the norms. Picture this: you walk into a meeting, and everyone is talking over each other, no one is listening, and the chaos is palpable. This scenario is the antithesis of a well-oiled machine, highlighting the importance of etiquette. Effective communication involves not just speaking clearly but also actively listening to others. It's about genuinely hearing your colleagues' words, considering their perspectives, and responding thoughtfully. This skill fosters an environment where ideas are exchanged freely and collaboration thrives. Equally important is respecting cultural and personal differences. In today's diverse workplaces, sensitivity to your coworkers' varied backgrounds and experiences enriches the team dynamic and enhances creativity.

Navigating workplace interactions can sometimes feel like a tightrope, but understanding common scenarios and how to respond can ease this tension. Receiving feedback is one such scenario. It can be challenging to hear criticism, but viewing it as an opportunity for growth is crucial. When a manager points out an area for improvement, listen carefully, ask clarifying questions if needed, and thank them for their insight. This approach not only demonstrates maturity but also shows your commitment to personal and professional development. Participating in meetings and discussions is another common workplace scenario. Here, contributing your ideas confidently while respecting others' contributions is key. If you disagree, do so respectfully, backing up your points with facts or experiences. This balanced engagement makes meetings more effective and ensures everyone feels valued.

Building positive relationships with colleagues is fundamental to creating a supportive professional network. Engaging in team-building activities is one way to strengthen these bonds. Such activities create opportunities to connect personally, fostering trust and understanding, whether it's a formal workshop or an informal lunch. Offering assistance and support is another way to build rapport. If a colleague is swamped with work, offering a helping hand or simply lending an ear can make a big difference. This generosity doesn't go unnoticed and often leads to reciprocal support when needed. These interactions cultivate a culture of teamwork and camaraderie, which is essential for a harmonious workplace.

Conflicts inevitably arise, even in the most favorable environments. However, constructively handling them is what maintains harmony. Mediation techniques can be invaluable in resolving disputes. Suggest a sit-down where everyone can voice their concerns without interruption if tensions flare. Acting as a neutral third party or involving a mediator can help keep the conversation productive and focused on solutions. Establishing common ground is another effective strategy. Find areas where you and your colleague agree, and build from there. This shared foundation can help bridge gaps and facilitate compromise, turning potential conflicts into opportunities for collaborative problem-solving. Understanding these dynamics and how to navigate them is critical to maintaining a peaceful and productive work environment. By focusing on communication, respect, and collaboration, you contribute to a workplace where everyone can thrive.

3.4 BUILDING A PROFESSIONAL NETWORK

Imagine entering a room buzzing with conversation, where every handshake could open a door to your future. Networking isn't just about collecting business cards; it's about building relationships that can lead to career opportunities and growth. In today's interconnected world, knowing the right people can be as valuable as having the right skills. Networking is not just about what you can gain but also about what you can offer. Before you start, identify your networking goals. Are you looking to learn from industry leaders, find a mentor, or discover job opportunities? Clear goals help you navigate the vast sea of professional connections more effectively. Industry events and conferences are ideal places to meet like-minded individuals. These gatherings provide a platform to engage with professionals who share your interests and can introduce you to new perspectives and possibilities.

The foundation of effective networking is a genuine connection. Crafting an elevator pitch is a crucial step. This brief, engaging introduction highlights who you are and what you're passionate about. It should be concise yet intriguing enough to spark further conversation. When you meet someone new, it's essential to follow up. A simple message or email thanking them for their time can go a long way in cementing the connection. Mention something specific from your conversation to remind them who you are and show that you were genuinely engaged. Following up enhances the initial interaction and sets the stage for a lasting relationship.

Social media plays a significant role in professional networking in the digital age. Platforms like LinkedIn are invaluable tools for enhancing your professional visibility. Optimizing your LinkedIn profile is the first step. Use a high-quality photo and write a compelling headline that reflects your career goals. Your summary should be a snapshot of your professional life, including key achievements and skills. Engaging with industry-related content is another way to increase your visibility. Share articles, comment on posts, and participate in discussions to position yourself as an active professional community member. This engagement keeps you informed and helps you connect with others who share your interests.

Maintaining and nurturing professional relationships requires effort and consistency. Regular check-ins and updates are essential to keep connections alive. This doesn't mean you need to contact everyone constantly, but a periodic message or meeting can keep the connection fresh. Offer value and support to your contacts whenever possible. This could be as simple as sharing an article that might interest them or introducing them to someone in your network who could help them. These small gestures build goodwill and strengthen your professional relationships. By focusing on mutual benefit rather than just personal gain, you create a network that is not only robust but also supportive and enriching.

3.5 NAVIGATING THE TRANSITION FROM COLLEGE TO CAREER

Stepping out of college and into the workforce can feel like you're suddenly thrust into a world with different rules and expectations. While your degree has armed you with knowledge, translating those academic skills into workplace competencies is another game. In college, you thrived on theory and essays. Still, it's about applying those theories to solve real problems in the workplace. For instance, group projects in college teach teamwork skills, but turning that into the ability to collaborate effectively with diverse teams in a professional setting is key. Understanding organizational structures further aids this transition. Companies have hierarchies, from entry-level positions to upper management, and knowing how these structures function helps you navigate office politics and understand where you fit into the bigger picture.

Managing expectations and setting career goals can help ease this transition. Often, fresh graduates enter the workforce with high expectations, dreaming of rapid promotions and accolades. While aiming high is excellent, setting realistic goals is also essential. Consider short-term plans that involve gaining experience and learning the ropes. At the same time, long-term goals might focus on climbing the career ladder or shifting into a dream role. Adapting to entry-level roles might mean handling tasks that feel mundane, but these roles are crucial. They lay the groundwork for understanding the industry and developing essential skills. Recognizing that these experiences are stepping stones can help maintain motivation and focus.

Continuous learning and development should be at the forefront of your career strategy. The world doesn't stand still, and neither should your skills. Pursuing certifications and attending workshops can keep you updated with industry trends and enhance your skill set. Whether learning a new software tool or developing leadership skills, these opportunities can set you apart. Seeking mentorship is another effective way to foster growth. A mentor can guide, share experiences, and offer insights you might not find in textbooks. They can also expand your network, introducing you to professionals who might open doors in the future.

The psychological shift from student to employee poses its own challenges, too. Balancing work-life dynamics is one such hurdle. Unlike college, where you have flexible schedules, a full-time job requires a more rigid routine. Finding time for social activities, hobbies, and relaxation is crucial to avoid burnout. Developing resilience is also essential. Mistakes are inevitable, but learning to bounce back and adapt matters. Each setback is a lesson in disguise, teaching you more about yourself and your capabilities.

These practical and psychological adjustments are part of the natural progression from college to career. They require patience, flexibility, and a willingness to learn, but mastering them sets the stage for a fulfilling professional life. As you become more comfortable in the workforce, these initial challenges will evolve into opportunities for growth, shaping your path in the professional world and beyond.

With these foundations, you're poised to tackle the complexities of personal finance, the next critical step in your adulting adventure.

CHAPTER 4

FINANCIAL FOUNDATIONS FOR YOUNG ADULTS

"Do not save what is left after spending, but spend what is left after saving."

— WARREN BUFFETT

Imagine this: You're at your favorite coffee shop, ready to order that caramel macchiato you've been craving all day. You open your digital wallet and see your balance dwindling faster than anticipated. Sound familiar? It's a small but telling reminder of how easy it is to lose track of your spending without a plan. And that's where budgeting comes in. Budgeting isn't about restricting yourself or cutting out every joy in life. It's about gaining control over your finances and ensuring your money works for you, not against you. A well-crafted budget is your blueprint for financial independence, setting the foundation for everything from paying off student loans to saving for a dream vacation.

4:1 BUILDING A BUDGET THAT WORKS FOR YOU

One practical approach to budgeting is zero-based budgeting, which means allocating every dollar of your income to expenses, savings, or debt repayment. The idea is simple: your income minus your expenses equals zero. This strategy forces you to account for every dollar, ensuring nothing slips through the cracks. On the other hand, the 50/30/20 rule offers a more flexible framework. Here, 50% of your income goes to needs like rent and groceries, 30% to wants like dining out or that macchiato, and 20% to savings and debt repayment. Choosing the correct method depends on your financial goals and lifestyle. Budgeting tools like Mint and YNAB (You Need A Budget) can make this process smoother. According to a review from NerdWallet, YNAB uses a zero-based budgeting approach, helping users plan for every dollar they earn. At the same time, Mint offers a comprehensive view of your finances by syncing with your bank accounts.

To create a personalized budget, list your fixed and variable expenses. Fixed expenses are those you can't change quickly, like rent or car payments. Variable costs, such as entertainment or dining out, fluctuate monthly. Identifying these categories helps you understand where your money goes. Next, set realistic financial goals. You may want to save for a new laptop or pay off that lingering credit card debt. Whatever your goals, make sure they're specific and achievable. Consider averaging your earnings over several months to create a consistent budget if your income is irregular. This approach provides a more stable financial picture, allowing you to plan effectively even when paychecks vary.

As you navigate budgeting, challenges like impulse spending can derail your progress. It's easy to get tempted by an impromptu night out or a flash sale online. To counteract this, establish strategies that work for you. It could be setting aside a small monthly amount for spontaneity or using cash instead of cards to limit spending. Tracking expenses is another hurdle many face. Regularly updating your budget with every expense, no matter how small, helps keep you accountable. Budgeting apps like PocketGuard simplify this process by providing a snapshot of your finances, showing how much money you have left after accounting for bills and goals. These apps are designed to support you and make the budgeting process less overwhelming.

Reviewing and adjusting your budget regularly is crucial to its success. Life changes, and so should your budget. Schedule monthly reviews to assess your spending habits and make necessary adjustments. Whether you've received a raise, moved to a new city, or faced unexpected expenses, your budget should reflect these changes. This practice helps you stay on track and provides insights into your financial behavior, allowing for more informed decisions. By regularly reviewing and adjusting your budget, you proactively manage your finances, ensuring that your budget remains relevant and practical. This proactive approach puts you in charge of your financial decisions and future.

Interactive Element: Monthly Budget Reflection Prompt

Take a moment at the end of each month to reflect on your budgeting journey. Ask yourself: What worked well this month? Where did I overspend, and why? What adjustments can I make for next month? Jot down your thoughts in a journal or note app. This habit encourages mindfulness and self-awareness, making budgeting a more engaging and insightful experience.

4.2 UNDERSTANDING CREDIT AND HOW TO BUILD IT

Think of credit as your financial reputation. It's a mirror that reflects how you handle money, and it's a key player in your financial well-being. Whether you're applying for a loan, renting an apartment, or signing up for a new phone plan, your credit score and report are in the spotlight. Your credit score, a three-digit number usually ranging from 300 to 850, predicts your likelihood of repaying borrowed money. The higher your score, the more trustworthy you appear to lenders. Your credit score can significantly influence major life decisions, making it essential to comprehend and manage it wisely.

Meanwhile, a credit report is a detailed history of your financial behavior, including your past and present credit accounts, payment history, and any outstanding debts. Lenders use this report to assess your creditworthiness. A strong credit score distinguishes between getting approved for a loan with a favorable interest rate. It affects both loan approvals and loan terms, such as the interest rate offered. On the other hand, a poor credit score can lead to higher interest rates, difficulty getting approved for loans, and even rejection of rental applications.

Building credit from scratch might seem daunting, but there are concrete steps you can take to establish a solid credit history. One method is to start with a secured credit card. This card type requires a cash deposit as collateral, which is your credit limit. Your credit limit is the maximum amount you can spend on the card without incurring debt. Because the risk is minimal for the lender, secured credit cards are often easier to obtain than traditional ones. Using this card responsibly—making small purchases and paying off the balance in full each month—helps build your credit history. Another strategy is becoming an authorized user on a family member's credit card. You can use their account, and your name gets added to their card. Their good credit behavior can positively influence your credit profile, provided they manage the account responsibly. This arrangement allows you to benefit from their established credit without the direct responsibility of the primary cardholder.

Maintaining a healthy credit score requires diligence and a few key habits. Paying your bills on time is crucial. Late payments can significantly damage your credit score and remain on your credit report for years. Setting up automatic payments or reminders ensures you never miss a due date. Another important factor is your credit utilization ratio, which is the percentage of your available credit you're using at any given time. Aim to keep this ratio below 30% to demonstrate responsible credit management. If you have a credit limit of $1,000, try not to carry a balance of more than $300. Regularly checking your credit report for errors can also safeguard your score. You're entitled to a free credit report annually from each of the three major bureaus—TransUnion, Equifax, and Experian—through AnnualCreditReport.com. Reviewing your report allows you to catch and dispute any inaccuracies that could negatively impact your score.

Misunderstandings about credit are common, but clearing these misconceptions is essential for effective credit management. One myth is that closing old accounts will improve your credit score. In reality, closing accounts can hurt your score by reducing your overall credit limit and increasing your utilization ratio. Additionally, long-standing accounts contribute to your credit history length, which is a factor in calculating your score. Another myth is that checking your credit score will lower it. While hard inquiries—like those made when applying for a new credit card—can impact your score slightly, checking your credit through a soft inquiry does not affect your score. In fact, regularly monitoring your credit is a good practice to maintain financial health and catch any signs of identity theft early. Understanding these nuances allows you to confidently navigate the world of credit and avoid common pitfalls.

4.3 SMART USE OF CREDIT CARDS AND AVOIDING DEBT

Credit cards can be a powerful tool for managing finances if used wisely. However, they demand a disciplined approach to avoid the pitfalls of debt. The first step in using credit cards responsibly is understanding the difference between needs and wants. Needs are essential expenses like rent, groceries, and utilities. Wants are discretionary, such as dining out or buying the latest gadget. By distinguishing between the two, you can make informed decisions about when to use your credit card and rely on other means like cash or debit. This clarity helps prevent impulsive purchases that can lead to debt accumulation. Rewards programs are another benefit of credit cards, offering perks like cashback, travel points, or discounts. These incentives can be enticing, but it's crucial to remember that they only benefit you if you pay off your balance in full each month. Otherwise, the interest accrued can outweigh any rewards earned.

Avoiding credit card debt requires a strategic approach to spending. Setting spending limits is a practical method to keep expenses in check. Determine a monthly limit that aligns with your budget and stick to it, treating your credit card like a debit card to avoid overspending. Balance transfer offers can be advantageous if you're managing existing debt. These offers typically allow you to transfer high-interest balances to a new card with a low or zero percent interest rate for a limited period. This can significantly reduce interest payments, but it's essential to understand the terms, including any fees for the transfer. Use this window wisely to pay the balance, as rates usually increase after the promotional period ends. Understanding these tools and techniques empowers you to manage your credit effectively, minimizing the risk of falling into debt.

Interest rates and fees are pivotal factors that can impact your financial health if not carefully managed. The Annual Percentage Rate (APR) represents the cost of borrowing on your credit card, expressed as a yearly interest rate. It's crucial to be aware of your card's APR, especially if you carry a balance, as it determines the interest charged on any unpaid amount. Navigating hidden fees is also essential. Some cards have annual fees, foreign transaction fees, or late payment fees. These can add up quickly, so read the fine print of your card agreement to understand what you might be liable for. Awareness of these costs helps you make informed decisions about which credit card to use and ensures you only incur necessary expenses.

If you find yourself in credit card debt, don't panic. There are effective strategies to help you regain control. The snowball method involves paying off your smallest debts first while making minimum payments on larger ones. This approach will boost your motivation as you see debts disappearing quickly. Alternatively, the avalanche method focuses on paying off debts with the highest interest rates first, potentially saving more money in the long run. Choose the method that best suits your financial situation and personal preferences. Seeking credit counseling services is another option. These professionals can provide guidance on managing debt, creating a budget, and negotiating with creditors. They will offer a fresh perspective and expert advice, helping you navigate the path to financial recovery.

Understanding the intricacies of credit card use, from managing expenses to handling debt, lays the foundation for a healthy financial future. By approaching credit with caution and knowledge, you can leverage its benefits while minimizing risks, paving the way for more excellent economic stability and peace of mind.

4.4 INTRODUCTION TO INVESTING AND SAVING FOR THE FUTURE

Picture this: your money is quietly growing while you sleep, thanks to the power of investing. It's not a distant dream but a practical reality, especially when you start early. Compound interest is at the heart of investing—a concept Albert Einstein famously called the world's eighth wonder. Essentially, it's the process where your investment earns interest, and then that interest earns even more interest. Over time, this can lead to exponential growth of your initial investment. Understanding this early can transform your financial future. Yet, investing isn't without its risks. Risk versus reward is fundamental; the potential for higher returns often involves more significant uncertainty. Balancing these elements is crucial, especially when you're just starting out.

Creating a solid savings and investment strategy begins with setting up an emergency fund. This fund acts as a financial cushion, providing security and peace of mind when unexpected expenses arise. Aim to save three to six months' worth of living expenses. Diversify your investment portfolio to spread risk once your emergency fund is in place. This means investing in a mix of assets like stocks, bonds, and real estate rather than putting all your money into one type. Diversification reduces the impact of poor performance in any single investment. Cryptocurrencies, like Bitcoin and Ethereum, have emerged as modern investment options. They offer the potential for high returns but come with volatility. Approach them cautiously, as a small part of a diversified portfolio, and view them as a hedge against traditional markets. Understanding these strategies helps build a balanced financial plan that aligns with your long-term goals.

Investment accounts come in various forms, each with its own benefits. A Roth IRA is a retirement account funded with after-tax dollars, allowing for tax-free growth and retirement withdrawal. It's an excellent choice if you expect to be in a higher tax bracket when you retire. In contrast, a Traditional IRA offers tax-deductible contributions, providing immediate tax benefits but taxed withdrawals in retirement. Choosing between the two depends on your current and expected future tax situations. Brokerage accounts are another option for investing in stocks, bonds, and mutual funds. They offer flexibility and access to a broad range of investments but lack the tax benefits of retirement accounts. Understanding these accounts and their implications can guide you in making informed decisions about your financial future.

Many young adults shy away from investing due to common misconceptions. One myth is that investing is only for the wealthy. In reality, platforms like Robinhood and Acorns have democratized investing, allowing you to start with as little as a few dollars. Investing isn't exclusive; it's accessible to anyone willing to learn and take calculated risks. Another myth is that stocks are too risky for beginners. While it's true that stocks can be volatile, they have historically offered higher returns over long periods than other investments. You can manage risk effectively by starting small, diversifying, and investing for the long term. By understanding and dispelling these myths, you can confidently approach investing, knowing it's a viable path to building wealth over time.

4.5 NAVIGATING TAXES WITH CONFIDENCE

Taxes are inevitable in adult life, often shrouded in mystery and apprehension. Yet, understanding them is crucial for financial health. At its core, the tax system is a mechanism through which governments fund public services like roads, schools, and healthcare. There are several types of taxes you may encounter. Income tax is the most familiar, levied on the money you earn from jobs, investments, and other sources. Sales tax is added to the price of goods and services, varying by location. Property tax is charged on real estate ownership, supporting local infrastructures like public schools and emergency services. Each type of tax serves a distinct purpose, contributing to the community and the country's broader economic stability. Understanding tax brackets is essential, as they determine the rate at which your income is taxed. The system is progressive, meaning the more you earn, the higher the percentage of tax you pay on income above a certain threshold.

Filing taxes doesn't have to be an intimidating task. It begins with gathering the necessary documents. If you're employed, your employer will provide a W-2 form detailing your earnings and taxes withheld. You'll receive a 1099 form for freelance or contract work, which outlines payments received. These documents are the foundation of your tax return. Next, you'll choose between the standard and itemized deductions. The standard deduction is a fixed amount that reduces your taxable income, while itemizing involves listing specific expenses—like medical costs or charitable contributions—that may exceed the standard deduction. The decision between the two depends on which method offers the more significant tax benefit. Once you've compiled your information and made these choices, you're ready to fill out your tax return, either manually or through tax software.

Young adults can benefit from numerous deductions and credits that reduce tax liability. The student loan interest deduction is valuable, allowing you to deduct interest paid on qualifying student loans, potentially lowering your taxable income by up to $2,500. Education credits, such as the American Opportunity Credit, offer further savings. This credit provides up to $2,500 per eligible student for tuition, fees, and course materials, helping offset the cost of higher education. Awareness of these options can lead to significant savings, making the tax system work for you rather than against you.

If the tax process feels overwhelming, numerous resources are available to assist you. Many free tax filing software options, like TurboTax or IRS Free File, guide you step-by-step through the process, ensuring accuracy and compliance. These programs often include checks for standard deductions and credits, maximizing your return. Professional tax services offer expert advice to those seeking personalized guidance. Tax professionals can navigate complex tax situations, provide strategic planning, and ensure you take full advantage of available deductions and credits. Whether you opt for software or professional help, the key is approaching tax season confidently, knowing that resources and support are readily accessible.

Navigating taxes might seem complex, but it's manageable with the right tools and knowledge. Understanding the basics of the tax system, knowing how to file correctly, and leveraging deductions and credits can ease the process. Taxes are a vital aspect of your financial foundation, and mastering them ensures you're prepared for the responsibilities and opportunities of adult life. As we move forward, let's explore how to maintain a healthy work-life balance, an equally important element in achieving well-rounded success.

CHAPTER 5

HEALTH AND WELLBEING MASTERY

"The greatest wealth is health."

— VIRGIL

Picture this: you've landed your first full-time job, and with it comes the daunting task of choosing a health insurance plan. Suddenly, you're faced with acronyms like HMO and PPO, which feel like deciphering a secret code. You're not alone in this confusion; navigating health insurance can be overwhelming. Understanding the different types of plans is crucial to making an informed choice that suits your needs and lifestyle.

5:1 CHOOSING THE RIGHT HEALTH INSURANCE PLAN

Health Maintenance Organization (HMO) plans typically offer lower monthly premiums but require you to select a primary care physician (PCP) and keep your healthcare within a specific network, a group of doctors, hospitals, and other healthcare providers contracted to provide services to plan members at a discounted rate. If you travel often or need specialist care, this can be limiting.

On the other hand, Preferred Provider Organization (PPO) plans provide more flexibility, allowing you to see any doctor without a referral, even out-of-network providers, albeit at a higher cost. High-deductible health plans (HDHPs) are another option, often paired with Health Savings Accounts (HSAs) to cover out-of-pocket expenses. These plans usually have lower premiums but require paying more upfront before coverage kicks in. Understanding these fundamental differences is the first step toward selecting a plan that aligns with your healthcare needs and financial situation, empowering you to make informed decisions about your health.

Choosing the right health insurance plan involves more than just comparing costs. It's essential to assess your healthcare needs thoroughly. Start by analyzing your personal health history. Do you have chronic conditions that require regular medication or specialist visits? If so, a plan with comprehensive coverage and lower out-of-pocket costs might be best. Consider your lifestyle and future healthcare needs as well. Are you planning to start a family or engage in activities that might increase your risk of injury? These factors should influence your decision, ensuring your plan covers anticipated medical expenses. The goal is to balance affordability and adequate coverage, providing peace of mind in knowing that you're prepared for routine and unexpected healthcare needs and that your resources are being used wisely.

When comparing insurance plans, it's crucial to look beyond the monthly premiums. Deductibles, copayments, and out-of-pocket maximums significantly determine the overall cost. A lower premium might seem attractive initially, but you could pay more in the long run if the deductible is high. Copayments, the fixed amounts you pay for services like doctor visits or prescriptions, also affect your expenses. Keep an eye on the network of doctors and hospitals included in the plan. If your preferred healthcare providers are out-of-network, you might face higher costs or have to switch doctors. A comprehensive comparison involves weighing these elements against your healthcare needs, ensuring that you choose a plan that offers both affordability and accessibility to quality care.

Common pitfalls can derail even the savviest insurance shopper. One major mistake is overlooking out-of-network costs. While a plan might cover most expenses within its network, out-of-network services can be significantly more expensive. This is especially important if you travel frequently or live in an area with limited in-network options. Another oversight is ignoring the annual out-of-pocket maximum, the most you'll have to pay during a policy period before your insurance covers 100% of costs. Reaching this maximum can offer relief in a year filled with medical expenses, but failing to consider it can lead to unexpected financial strain. Knowing these potential pitfalls helps you avoid costly surprises and select a plan that meets your needs.

Interactive Element: Health Insurance Plan Comparison Checklist

As you navigate your options, consider creating a "Health Insurance Plan Comparison Checklist." Include categories like monthly premiums, deductibles, copayments, network coverage, and out-of-pocket maximums. Use this checklist to evaluate each plan, ensuring a thorough comparison that aligns with your healthcare needs and budget. This methodical approach can simplify decision-making, providing clarity and confidence as you choose a plan.

5.2 DENTAL, VISION, AND PREVENTATIVE HEALTHCARE BASICS

Imagine waking up one morning feeling healthy and energized, ready to tackle the day. This scenario is not just luck but often due to diligent preventative care. Regular check-ups and screenings are crucial in maintaining health and catching potential issues early. Annual physical exams, for instance, serve as a comprehensive assessment of your overall health, allowing your doctor to monitor vital signs, discuss lifestyle habits, and update vaccinations. Preventative care also includes regular screenings for conditions like high blood pressure, cholesterol, and diabetes and lifestyle changes like maintaining a healthy diet and regular exercise. Keeping up with vaccinations and immunizations is crucial, as they protect against preventable diseases and can significantly reduce the risk of outbreaks in communities. These preventative measures are not merely routine but pivotal steps in safeguarding your health, ensuring you can continue to lead an active and fulfilling life without the looming threat of undetected health problems.

Dental health is another cornerstone of overall wellbeing. Regular dental check-ups are essential, typically recommended every six months, as they allow your dentist to clean your teeth, check for cavities, and screen for oral diseases like gingivitis or oral cancer. Proper brushing and flossing techniques at home can prevent plaque buildup and cavities. Use a fluoride toothpaste and a toothbrush with soft bristles, brushing at least twice daily. Floss daily to remove food particles and plaque from between your teeth, which your toothbrush can't reach. These habits are simple yet effective ways to maintain oral health and prevent more severe dental issues, saving you from discomfort and costly procedures.

Vision care often takes a backseat until problems arise, but it's a crucial element of health maintenance. Regular eye exams are essential, usually every one to two years, even if you don't wear glasses or contact lenses. These exams can detect vision changes and uncover eye conditions that might not show symptoms initially, such as glaucoma or macular degeneration. In today's digital age, reducing digital eye strain is increasingly important. Consider the 20-20-20 rule: for every 20 minutes spent looking at a screen, look at something 20 feet away for at least 20 seconds. This practice, adjusting screen brightness and using blue light filters, can help reduce digital eye strain and protect your eyes, enhancing your comfort and productivity, whether you're working, studying, or gaming.

Preventative services are powerful tools in maintaining health and preventing more serious conditions. Cholesterol and blood pressure screenings are vital, especially as you age, even if you feel fine. High blood pressure and high cholesterol often have no symptoms. Still, they can lead to serious issues like heart disease and stroke if left unchecked. Regular cancer screenings, such as mammograms and colonoscopies, are equally crucial for early detection and successful treatment outcomes. These tests can catch cancer in its early stages when it's most treatable, significantly increasing survival rates. Utilizing these services, often covered by insurance, is an investment in your health, offering peace of mind and the opportunity to address potential health issues before they escalate.

Reflection Section: Personal Preventative Health Checklist

Consider creating a "Personal Preventative Health Checklist" to track your regular check-ups, screenings, and vaccinations. This checklist can serve as a reminder for upcoming appointments and help you stay on top of your health. Regularly updating and reviewing this checklist ensures that you're actively participating in your healthcare, making informed decisions, and taking proactive steps to maintain your wellbeing.

Engaging in regular preventative health measures may seem like a lot of effort. Still, they are vital for sustaining and enhancing your quality of life. They allow you to catch potential health issues early and maintain your physical condition, enabling you to focus on pursuing your passions and enjoying life.

5.3 THE ART OF MINDFULNESS AND MEDITATION FOR STRESS MANAGEMENT

Imagine a moment when your mind feels clear, and your stress seems to drift away like clouds after a storm. This is the power of mindfulness, which invites you to be fully present in each moment. Mindfulness can be a game-changer for mental health, helping to reduce anxiety and stress while enhancing focus and concentration. Paying attention to your thoughts and feelings without judgment creates a space where stressors lose their grip. This practice encourages a calm and centered approach to life's challenges, allowing you to respond thoughtfully rather than impulsively. In a world where distractions are constant, mindfulness offers a refuge, a way to reconnect with yourself and find balance amidst chaos.

Starting a meditation practice might seem daunting at first, but it's simpler than you might think. Begin by finding a quiet space where you won't be disturbed. This could be a corner of your room or a peaceful spot in a nearby park. Sit comfortably on a cushion or chair, keeping your back straight to help with focus and relaxation. Close your eyes gently and bring your attention to your breath. Notice the sensation of air entering and leaving your nostrils or the rise and fall of your chest. If your mind wanders, gently guide it to your breath without frustration. Start with just five minutes a day, gradually increasing the time as you become more comfortable. This daily practice can enrich your life in unexpected ways, offering a grounding experience that nurtures both mind and body.

Mindfulness isn't confined to sitting still; it can be woven into the fabric of your daily life through various techniques. Mindful eating, for instance, transforms meals into a sensory experience. Rather than rushing through lunch with one eye on your phone, take a moment to appreciate the colors, textures, and flavors of your food. This practice not only enhances enjoyment but can also lead to healthier eating habits. Walking meditation is another way to incorporate mindfulness into your routine. As you walk, focus on the sensation of your feet touching the ground, the rhythm of your steps, and the sights and sounds around you. This moving meditation can bring peace and clarity, turning a simple walk into a rejuvenating exercise for the mind.

Real-life applications of mindfulness demonstrate its versatility and practicality. In the workplace, mindfulness can improve productivity and job satisfaction. Taking a few moments to center yourself before a meeting can enhance focus and communication, leading to more effective collaboration. Mindfulness also aids in managing emotions during challenging situations. Whether navigating a conflict with a friend or dealing with unexpected setbacks, mindfulness helps you remain calm and composed. By observing your emotions without being swept away by them, you gain the clarity needed to handle difficulties with grace. This practice fosters resilience, offering a toolkit for navigating life's inevitable ups and downs confidently and calmly.

5.4 THE IMPORTANCE OF SLEEP AND HOW TO OPTIMIZE IT

Imagine waking up feeling refreshed, your mind sharp and ready to tackle the day. Sleep is not just a daily ritual; it's a cornerstone of health, affecting both your body and mind. When you sleep well, your immune system is at its best, ready to fend off illnesses. This is because, during sleep, your body produces cytokines, proteins essential for fighting infection and inflammation. If you skimp on sleep, your body's ability to make these protective proteins decreases, leaving you more vulnerable to viruses and germs. Beyond the physical, sleep has a profound impact on mental health. During these restful hours, your brain processes emotions and memories, contributing to emotional stability. Lack of sleep, on the other hand, can exacerbate mental health issues like anxiety and depression, creating a cycle of exhaustion and stress.

Improving your sleep quality begins with establishing a consistent bedtime routine. Your body thrives on regularity, so going to bed and waking up at the same time each day helps regulate your internal clock. Consider winding down with calming activities like reading or taking a warm bath. These habits signal your body that it's time to relax and prepare for sleep. Creating a sleep-conducive environment is also crucial. Keep your bedroom cool, quiet, and dark to promote restful slumber. Invest in blackout curtains if outside light disrupts your sleep, and consider using a white noise machine to mask disruptive sounds. These small changes can make your bedroom a sanctuary for rest, enhancing the quality of your sleep.

Sleep disorders, though familiar, often go unrecognized. Insomnia, characterized by difficulty falling or staying asleep, can be a temporary or chronic problem. Pay attention to signs like persistent fatigue, irritability, or difficulty concentrating, which may indicate insomnia. Sleep apnea is another disorder to be aware of—a condition where breathing repeatedly stops and starts during sleep. Symptoms include loud snoring, gasping for air during sleep, and excessive daytime sleepiness. If you suspect you have a sleep disorder, consult a healthcare provider. Treatments range from lifestyle changes and therapies to medical interventions like Continuous Positive Airway Pressure (CPAP) machines for sleep apnea.

In our tech-driven world, balancing technology use with healthy sleep habits is more important than ever. The blue light emitted by screens can interfere with your body's production of melatonin, a hormone that regulates sleep. Limiting screen time before bed is a simple yet effective strategy to improve sleep. Aim to power down devices at least an hour before bedtime. If you need to use your phone or computer, consider using blue light filters or apps that reduce blue light exposure. Sleep-tracking apps can also be beneficial, offering insights into your sleep patterns. These tools can help you identify trends and make adjustments to improve your sleep quality. However, don't let these apps become a source of stress—use them as guides, not gospel.

Incorporating these strategies into your daily life can transform your sleep experience, enhancing your physical and mental wellbeing. With quality sleep, you're better equipped to face challenges, seize opportunities, and enjoy life's moments with clarity and vigor.

5.5 EXERCISE ESSENTIALS FOR A BALANCED LIFESTYLE

You do more than move your body when you lace up your sneakers and step out for a run. Regular physical activity is a powerhouse for both physical and mental health. Exercise enhances cardiovascular health by strengthening your heart, lowering blood pressure, and improving circulation. These benefits contribute to a reduced risk of heart disease and stroke, pivotal for a long, healthy life. But that's not all. The endorphins released during exercise act as natural mood boosters, lifting your spirits and increasing your energy levels. This can translate into a more positive outlook and greater resilience in facing life's challenges. A consistent workout routine can even help manage stress, anxiety, and depression, offering a natural remedy that enhances overall wellbeing.

Creating a personalized exercise routine starts with setting realistic fitness goals. These goals should reflect your lifestyle, preferences, and current fitness level. If you're new to exercise, begin with achievable targets, like walking for 20 minutes thrice a week.

As you progress, gradually increase the intensity and duration of your workouts. Incorporate a mix of cardiovascular exercises, strength training, and flexibility work to ensure a well-rounded routine. Cardio activities like running, cycling, or swimming improve endurance and heart health. Strength training, using weights or bodyweight exercises, builds muscle and bone density, which is crucial for maintaining metabolism and preventing injuries. Flexibility exercises, such as stretching or yoga, enhance mobility, posture, and balance, helping prevent strains and injuries.

Staying motivated to exercise regularly can be challenging, but there are ways to keep the momentum going. Finding a workout buddy can make all the difference. This person can offer accountability, encouragement, and companionship, transforming exercise from a solitary task into a social event. Additionally, tracking progress with fitness apps can be highly motivating. Apps like MyFitnessPal or Fitbit enable you to set goals, monitor achievements, and visualize your progress over time. They provide reminders, tips, and even virtual badges for reaching milestones, making exercise more engaging and rewarding. Celebrating small victories reinforces positive habits, keeping you on track toward your fitness aspirations.

Exploring different types of physical activities can keep your routine fresh and exciting, preventing boredom and plateauing. Yoga and Pilates are excellent for building flexibility and core strength. These practices encourage mindfulness and breath control, offering mental clarity alongside physical benefits. Group sports and recreational activities also provide a dynamic way to stay fit. Whether joining a local soccer team, participating in a dance class, or trying rock climbing, these activities foster teamwork and camaraderie while providing a comprehensive workout.

They also introduce an element of fun and challenge, encouraging you to push your limits and try new things.

As we wrap up this chapter on health and wellbeing, remember that a balanced lifestyle is about integrating these practices into everyday life, supporting physical and mental health. Exercise is more than a routine; it's a foundation for vitality and happiness. Ready to move forward? In the next chapter, we'll explore how to master professional development and career success.

MAKE A DIFFERENCE

"The best way to find yourself is to lose yourself in the service of others."

— *MAHATMA GANDHI*

Hey there!

Thank you so much for picking up *The Ultimate Adulting Guide*! We hope you're enjoying learning how to navigate this crazy thing called adulthood. Whether it's learning how to manage money, write a killer resume, or figure out how to cook a meal without setting off the fire alarm, this book is here to help guide you through it all.

But we need your help! If you've found any of the advice in the book useful (or even if you just had a good laugh reading it), we'd love for you to share your thoughts with others.

Here's how you can help:

1. **Leave a Review:** Your opinion matters! By sharing your honest review, you're helping others who might be unsure if this book is right for them. Plus, it lets us know what parts of the book you loved (and maybe which parts we can improve for the next edition).
2. **Spread the Word:** Have a friend or family member about to enter adulthood? Let them know about the guide! Adulting doesn't have to be stressful, and *The Ultimate Adulting Guide* can be their secret weapon.

3. **What to Include:** Feel free to share any favorite tips or ideas from the book. Did the budgeting tips save you money? Did the resume advice help you land a job interview? Or the meal prep ideas made dinner time a breeze. We want to hear about your real-life experiences.

How to leave a review: It's simple! Just go to wherever you bought the book—Amazon, Goodreads, etc. or scan the QR code and leave your honest thoughts. Your feedback helps others find the right tools to adult like a pro.

Thanks again for reading *The Ultimate Adulting Guide*. We're excited to hear your thoughts and continue helping you become the best adult you can be!

Best,

Janine DeSimone

Author of *The Ultimate Adulting Guide*

CHAPTER 6

RELATIONSHIP MANAGEMENT AND COMMUNICATION SKILLS

"Communication is the key to understanding and resolving any conflict."

— UNKNOWN

Imagine this: you're catching up with a friend over coffee, and while they're sharing a story, your mind drifts to the text message you forgot to send or the endless to-do list waiting for you at home. It's a common scenario where communication falters, and despite your best intentions, you might miss the essence of what they're saying. Effective communication is the cornerstone of any relationship, yet it's often more challenging than it appears. This chapter explores how mastering communication skills can enhance your connections, making them more meaningful and fulfilling.

6:1 EFFECTIVE COMMUNICATION IN PERSONAL RELATIONSHIPS

Active listening, the cornerstone of effective communication, is a skill that involves genuinely hearing and understanding the other person. It requires being fully present, focusing entirely on the speaker, and avoiding distractions. This means putting away your phone, making eye contact, and using non-verbal cues like nodding to show engagement. Being fully present signals to the speaker that their words matter. Another vital technique is asking open-ended questions, encouraging the speaker to elaborate and share more depth. This approach not only shows genuine interest but also strengthens the bond between you. Reflecting or paraphrasing what the speaker has said confirms your understanding and validates the speaker's emotions, fostering empathy and connection. This combination of techniques helps you build trust and understanding, empowering you to offer support and empathy.

Straightforward and assertive communication is essential for expressing your thoughts and feelings effectively. Assertive communication involves expressing your needs confidently while respecting others' rights and opinions. Using "I" statements is one way to do this, as they focus on your feelings and needs without blaming or criticizing others. For example, saying, "I feel overwhelmed when plans change at the last minute," is more constructive than "You always change plans." This assertive yet respectful approach fosters open dialogue and prevents defensiveness. Balancing assertiveness with respect means being clear about what you need and being open to others' perspectives. It involves an assertive yet non-aggressive tone, maintaining direct eye contact, and using appropriate facial expressions. These characteristics enhance mutual respect and understanding, creating a foundation for healthier relationships.

Communication barriers can often hinder understanding, but with the right strategies, you can overcome them. Misunderstandings are common obstacles, frequently arising from assumptions or misinterpretations. When you encounter a misunderstanding, address it promptly by seeking clarification. Ask questions to ensure you've grasped the intended message and avoid jumping to conclusions. Managing non-verbal cues effectively is another key aspect. Body language, such as crossed arms or avoiding eye contact, can convey unintended messages, so being mindful of your non-verbal signals is crucial. Observing others' non-verbal cues can also provide insights into their feelings and thoughts, helping you adjust your responses accordingly. By focusing on these strategies, you can navigate communication barriers and foster deeper connections.

Open and honest dialogue is the glue that holds relationships together, maintaining trust and respect. Creating a safe space for difficult conversations is vital. This means establishing an environment where both parties feel comfortable sharing their thoughts without fear of judgment or retribution. Encourage feedback and reflection by inviting others to share their thoughts and experiences. This openness not only strengthens the relationship but also promotes personal growth. Being transparent in your communication builds trust, ensuring that both parties feel valued and respected. By prioritizing open and honest dialogue, you cultivate resilient and enduring relationships, capable of weathering challenges and celebrating successes together.

Reflection Section: Communication Self-Assessment

Consider taking a moment to reflect on your communication habits. Ask yourself: Do I actively listen or find my mind wandering during conversations? Do I express my needs clearly and respectfully, or do I shy away from confrontation? How do I handle misunderstandings—do I seek clarification or let assumptions linger? Jot down your thoughts and identify areas for growth. This self-assessment encourages mindfulness and continuous improvement, enhancing your ability to connect and communicate effectively.

6.2 SETTING BOUNDARIES AND MAINTAINING THEM

In any relationship, boundaries are like invisible lines that keep us balanced, allowing us to maintain our personal wellbeing while engaging with others. They're essential because they create a space where you can be yourself without feeling overwhelmed or taken for granted. Imagine a friend who constantly borrows your things without asking, leaving you feeling frustrated and disrespected. Setting boundaries helps prevent such scenarios, protecting your emotional and mental health. It starts with identifying your personal limits and needs. Consider what makes you comfortable or uncomfortable, and think about past experiences where you felt your boundaries were crossed. These reflections help you understand your needs, guiding you in establishing clear boundaries necessary for healthy relationships.

Communicating these boundaries effectively is crucial. It involves articulating them clearly and respectfully, ensuring others understand your limits without feeling accused or attacked. Using assertive language is key here. It's about expressing your needs directly and confidently, without aggression. For instance, saying, "I need some alone time to recharge after work," sets a clear boundary without blaming others. When discussing boundaries, approach it as a negotiation rather than a demand. This means being open to compromise and understanding the other person's perspective. Mutual respect is vital, fostering cooperation and ensuring that both parties feel heard and valued. By communicating boundaries in this manner, you create an environment of understanding and respect where everyone knows what to expect and can interact harmoniously.

Maintaining boundaries is often more challenging than setting them, but it's crucial for your emotional well-being. Upholding them consistently requires vigilance and self-awareness. Recognizing boundary violations is the first step. Being aware of instances where your boundaries are being tested or ignored is crucial. When this happens, respond assertively but calmly. Reiterate your boundary and explain why it's essential. For example, if a colleague repeatedly interrupts your work with non-urgent issues, remind them of your need for focused time and suggest scheduling a specific time to discuss non-urgent matters. Addressing violations promptly prevents them from becoming habitual, safeguarding your wellbeing and reinforcing boundaries. Consistency is key, reinforcing your commitment to maintaining your personal space and needs.

Setting boundaries can be uncomfortable, especially if you're new to it or fear how others will react. It's common to feel guilt or face pushback when asserting your needs. Overcoming this discomfort involves recognizing that setting boundaries is not selfish; it's a necessary act of self-care. To cope with guilt, remember that respecting your needs is essential for maintaining healthy relationships. It's okay to prioritize your wellbeing. Facing resistance from others can be daunting, but staying firm and reiterating your boundaries helps reinforce their importance. Seeking support from peers or mentors can provide valuable encouragement and advice. They can share their experiences and offer guidance on handling difficult situations, boosting your confidence in maintaining your boundaries.

Interactive Element: Boundary Reflection Exercise

Take a moment to reflect on your personal boundaries. Ask yourself: What situations make me uncomfortable, and why? How can I articulate these boundaries clearly? Write down your thoughts and identify two or three boundaries you want to establish or reinforce. Consider how you'll communicate them and anticipate any challenges you might face. This exercise encourages clarity and preparation, empowering you to set and maintain boundaries confidently.

6.3 MANAGING CONFLICT AND FINDING RESOLUTIONS

Conflict is an inevitable aspect of any relationship, like seasonal changes. It's not necessarily a bad thing; in fact, it can be a catalyst for growth and understanding if handled well. Imagine a disagreement with a friend or partner not as a battleground but as a chance to learn and improve. Differentiating between constructive and destructive conflict is key. Constructive conflict focuses on resolution and understanding, whereas destructive conflict spirals into blame and resentment. Recognizing which type of conflict you're facing allows you to approach it with a mindset geared toward positive outcomes. For instance, a disagreement about shared responsibilities at home can be an opportunity to clarify expectations and improve cooperation rather than letting resentment build. This perspective shift transforms conflicts from potential relationship breakers into opportunities for strengthening bonds.

Effective conflict resolution hinges on collaborative problem-solving and compromise. It's about working together to find a solution that satisfies both parties rather than insisting on your own way. Collaborative problem-solving involves listening to each other's perspectives and brainstorming solutions that address the needs of everyone involved. This approach fosters a sense of teamwork and equality, making it easier to reach a consensus. Compromise plays a crucial role here, requiring both parties to give a little to gain a lot. It's not about winning or losing but finding a middle ground where both feel valued and heard. Consensus-building, meanwhile, encourages open dialogue and shared decision-making, ensuring that the resolution is mutual and sustainable. These techniques resolve the immediate issue and build a stronger foundation for future interactions, enhancing trust and collaboration.

Managing emotions during conflict is another vital skill that can transform disagreements into productive discussions. Emotional regulation involves recognizing your feelings and controlling your reactions, ensuring that emotions don't hijack the conversation. Staying calm and focused allows you to address the issue without letting anger or frustration take over. Techniques such as taking deep breaths, pausing before responding, and reminding yourself of the bigger picture can help maintain composure. When you feel emotions rising, it's okay to take a break and return to the discussion once you're calmer. This practice prevents escalation and keeps the conversation productive. By controlling your emotions, you set the tone for a respectful exchange, encouraging the other person to mirror your calmness and approach the conflict with an open mind.

Reflecting on conflicts after they occur is a valuable exercise that can lead to personal growth and improved interactions. Analyzing conflict patterns helps identify recurring issues and underlying causes, providing insights into how you can approach similar situations differently in the future. You may notice that disagreements often arise from miscommunications or unvoiced expectations. With this knowledge, you can focus on improving communication or setting more explicit expectations. Implementing changes based on these reflections ensures that conflicts become learning experiences, not just points of contention. This proactive approach turns past disagreements into stepping stones for better future interactions, enhancing your ability to navigate conflicts gracefully and understanding. By viewing conflicts as opportunities for growth, you improve your relationships and develop a deeper understanding of yourself and others, fostering more harmonious and fulfilling connections.

6.4 NAVIGATING ROMANTIC RELATIONSHIPS WITH EMOTIONAL INTELLIGENCE

In the realm of romantic relationships, emotional intelligence acts as a guiding light, enhancing connections by fostering more profound understanding and empathy. At its core, emotional intelligence is about recognizing, understanding, and managing your own emotions, as well as perceiving and empathizing with your partner's emotions. Imagine you're in a situation where your partner seems distant and withdrawn. Instead of reacting defensively, you pause to consider what they might be feeling or experiencing. This awareness allows you to approach the situation with compassion rather than judgment. Emotional intelligence enriches romantic relationships by creating a space where both partners feel seen and understood, laying the groundwork for a stronger, more resilient bond.

Developing emotional intelligence begins with practicing emotional self-awareness—recognizing and understanding your emotions and their impact on your thoughts and actions. Start by considering how you feel in different situations and how these feelings influence your behavior. Journaling can be a helpful tool here, allowing you to reflect on your emotions and identify patterns over time. As you become more attuned to your feelings, you'll find it easier to manage them, preventing emotional reactions from clouding your judgment. Another aspect of emotional intelligence is empathy, which involves understanding and sharing your partner's feelings. Practice empathy by putting yourself in their shoes and considering their perspective and emotions. This practice deepens your connection and fosters a sense of partnership and mutual support.

Mutual respect and support are the pillars of any healthy romantic relationship. They create a foundation of trust where both partners feel valued and appreciated. Imagine building a house—trust is the solid foundation that supports everything else. Without it, the structure is unstable and fragile. In relationships, trust develops through consistent actions and words that demonstrate reliability and honesty. Showing appreciation for your partner's efforts, big and small, reinforces this trust. Whether it's acknowledging their hard work or expressing gratitude for their support, these actions strengthen your bond. Collaborative goal-setting is another way to nurture mutual respect and support. Working together towards shared objectives creates a sense of teamwork and unity. It could be as simple as planning a future vacation or as complex as making long-term financial plans. These shared goals reinforce your commitment to each other, fostering a deeper connection.

Navigating relationship challenges is crucial, as every relationship encounters bumps along the way. One common challenge is differences in values or goals, which can lead to misunderstandings or disagreements. When faced with these differences, approach them with an open mind and willingness to find common ground. This might involve compromise or adjusting expectations, but the effort is worthwhile for the relationship's health. Jealousy and trust issues are another hurdle many couples face. Addressing these issues requires honesty and vulnerability. If you feel jealous, communicate your feelings to your partner openly, explaining why you think this way without placing blame. Trust is built over time through transparency and consistent actions, so be patient and understanding. These challenges may test your relationship, but they also offer opportunities for growth and learning.

Emotional intelligence acts as a compass in romantic relationships, guiding you through the complexities of connection and intimacy. By honing your emotional awareness and empathy, you create a nurturing environment where mutual respect and support thrive. This foundation empowers you to face challenges with resilience and understanding, strengthening your bond and enriching your shared journey.

6.5 BUILDING LASTING FRIENDSHIPS

Friendships are the quiet yet profound threads that weave through the fabric of our lives, offering both support and joy. They're the people you turn to when you need a laugh, a shoulder to cry on, or simply someone to share a moment with. A diverse social network enriches your life, bringing various perspectives and experiences that broaden your understanding of the world. Friends from different backgrounds offer insights into cultures and lifestyles different from your own, which can be both enlightening and humbling. This diversity also fosters empathy and tolerance, essential in today's interconnected world. Friendships aren't just about having fun; they're integral to your wellbeing, providing emotional support that helps you navigate life's ups and downs.

Forming and maintaining meaningful connections might seem daunting, especially if you're stepping into a new environment, but it's entirely achievable with some effort and openness. Start by finding common interests and activities. Common ground paves the way for deeper connections, whether it's a shared love for hiking, a weekly trivia night, or a mutual appreciation for the latest Netflix series. Joining clubs or groups that align with your interests can introduce you to like-minded individuals. Nurturing them through regular communication is key once you've formed these initial connections. A quick message to check in, a funny meme shared over social media, or a spontaneous coffee date can keep friendships vibrant and alive. These small gestures show that you value the relationship and are willing to invest time and energy into it, strengthening the bond you share.

Friendships, like any relationship, are not without their challenges. Misunderstandings or conflicts can arise, but handling them with care can prevent them from damaging the friendship. When misunderstandings occur, address them directly and calmly. Open a dialogue to express your feelings and listen to your friend's perspective. Often, simple miscommunications can be resolved with a bit of patience and understanding. Balancing time and attention between friendships can also be tricky, especially when life gets busy. It's essential to prioritize your friendships without neglecting your own needs. Scheduling regular catch-ups or setting aside specific times for friends helps maintain the connection without overwhelming your schedule. Recognizing that friendships ebb and flow is crucial, allowing you to navigate these dynamics without unnecessary stress.

Surrounding yourself with positive influences is essential for fostering a supportive social circle. Seek out individuals who inspire you, challenge you, and encourage you to grow. Building a community of like-minded people creates an environment where mutual growth and learning are celebrated. This doesn't mean everyone must think or act the same, but rather that there's a shared respect and appreciation for each other's journeys. Encouraging mutual growth in friendships involves supporting each other's goals and celebrating achievements, no matter how small. This support network becomes a source of strength, providing encouragement and motivation when needed. These friendships become more than just social connections; they evolve into a community where you feel supported and empowered to pursue your passions.

As this chapter concludes, the focus shifts towards building friendships that enrich your life with support, joy, and growth. The next chapter will explore social etiquette and cultural competence, diving deeper into how these elements shape interactions within diverse environments.

CHAPTER 7

SOCIAL ETIQUETTE AND CULTURAL COMPETENCE

"The highest form of wisdom is kindness."

— THE TALMUD

Imagine you're at a wedding reception, surrounded by people you've never met, and the air is filled with clinking glasses and laughter. You glance around, noticing how effortlessly some guests glide from conversation to conversation. In contrast, others linger awkwardly at the room's edges. Social etiquette in these settings is like the invisible thread that holds the tapestry of interactions together, ensuring everyone feels welcomed and respected. It's a subtle art that, when mastered, empowers you to navigate gatherings with confidence and grace.

7:1 SOCIAL ETIQUETTE IN GROUP EVENTS AND GATHERINGS

Etiquette isn't about rigid rules or outdated formality; it's about treating those around you with consideration and kindness, fostering an environment where everyone can enjoy the moment without friction or faux pas.

Understanding the role of a host or guest is fundamental to participating in social events. As a host, your responsibilities extend beyond organizing the venue and refreshments. You're the one who sets the tone for the gathering, ensuring guests feel comfortable and engaged. This might mean introducing newcomers to others, initiating conversations, or simply being attentive to the needs of your guests. Meanwhile, as a guest, you reciprocate the host's efforts by being courteous and appreciative. Arriving on time, thanking the host, and mingling with other guests are small acts that show respect and gratitude. Moreover, respecting event-specific customs and traditions is crucial, whether toasting the bride and groom at a wedding or observing quiet moments at a memorial service. These practices, rooted in cultural or familial significance, uphold the spirit and purpose of the gathering.

In any event, appropriate behavior can significantly enhance your social experience. Dress codes, for instance, communicate respect for the occasion and its participants. While a formal event might call for suits and elegant dresses, a casual gathering could be more relaxed, welcoming jeans and sneakers. Paying attention to the invitation or asking the host can prevent awkwardness and ensure you're dressed suitably. Once at the event, engaging in conversation requires a balance of openness and discretion. Though often undervalued, small talk is a powerful tool for breaking the ice and forging connections. Topics like the weather, recent movies, or shared interests are safe starting points. However, steering clear of controversial subjects such as politics or religion is advisable unless you're confident the conversation will remain light-hearted and respectful.

Group dynamics can be intricate, especially in larger gatherings where multiple conversations co-occur. Active listening is a skill that can elevate your participation in group discussions. It involves more than just hearing words; it's about understanding the speaker's intent and responding thoughtfully. You show that you value the other person's contribution by nodding, maintaining eye contact, and asking pertinent questions. This level of engagement can foster inclusivity and mutual respect, making everyone feel more connected.

Networking within social gatherings allows you to expand your personal and professional circles while maintaining etiquette. Introducing yourself and others politely can set the stage for meaningful connections. A simple, "Hi, I'm [Your Name], and I work in [Your Field]. How about you?" can open doors to engaging exchanges. When introducing others, briefly mention something they have in common, such as shared interests or mutual acquaintances, to facilitate conversation. Following up with new acquaintances after the event is crucial in building lasting relationships. A quick message or email expressing gratitude for the interaction can reinforce the connection. This proactive approach demonstrates genuine interest in maintaining contact and can lead to more meaningful relationships.

Interactive Element: Conversation Starter Checklist

Create your own "Conversation Starter Checklist" for different social settings. Include topics like recent books or movies, hobbies, or travel experiences. Practice these with friends to gain confidence. This tool will help you avoid awkward silences and keep conversations flowing naturally.

In embracing social etiquette, you're not merely adhering to conventions but enhancing the human experience. With consideration and thoughtfulness, you can navigate any social setting with poise, leaving a lasting positive impression wherever you go.

7:2 NAVIGATING CULTURAL DIFFERENCES WITH SENSITIVITY

You find yourself in a bustling market in a foreign city, surrounded by the sounds of unfamiliar languages and the aromas of exotic foods. As you try to communicate with a vendor, you realize that the gestures you use at home mean something entirely different here. This moment captures the essence of cultural competence, which is crucial in our increasingly interconnected world. Understanding and respecting cultural differences can transform interactions from awkward to rewarding, bridging gaps that language alone cannot. While often innocent, cultural misunderstandings can lead to unintended offense or isolation. For instance, a simple thumbs-up, which signals approval in some cultures, is considered rude in others. Such missteps can hinder relationships and create barriers where no need exists. Yet, embracing cultural exchange enriches our lives, offering new perspectives and fostering a deeper appreciation for diversity. Diversity isn't just about differences; it's a mosaic of experiences that, when understood, lead to innovation and empathy. Therefore, it's crucial to be culturally competent to avoid such misunderstandings and foster positive relationships.

Increasing cultural awareness requires proactive effort. Begin by learning about cultural norms and practices, not just superficially, but with genuine curiosity. For instance, in some cultures, it's customary to remove your shoes before entering a home, while in others, it's polite to leave them on. Read books, watch documentaries, or attend workshops on different cultures. These resources offer insights into traditions, values, and everyday behaviors that define a culture. Recognizing and challenging personal biases is equally vital. We all harbor preconceived notions shaped by our upbringing and environment. Reflecting on these biases and questioning their validity can open doors to fully understanding others. Engage in conversations with people from various backgrounds and truly listen to their stories. These interactions can enlighten, challenge your views, and broaden your horizons. By immersing yourself in diverse narratives, you develop a richer, more nuanced world perspective.

Effective communication is the linchpin in bridging cultural gaps. Using inclusive language, free of jargon or assumptions, ensures your message is clear and respectful. Avoid idioms or phrases that might not translate well across cultures. Instead, opt for straightforward language that conveys your intentions without ambiguity. Adapting your communication style to different cultural contexts shows respect and willingness to connect on a deeper level. For example, some cultures value directness, while others prefer indirect communication to maintain harmony. Being mindful of these preferences can prevent misunderstandings and promote mutual respect. Please pay attention to non-verbal cues, such as body language and eye contact, as they vary significantly between cultures. A gesture as simple as a handshake can hold different meanings and levels of acceptability, depending on the cultural backdrop.

Openness and curiosity towards different cultures are the keys to embracing diversity. Participating in cultural events and festivals allows you to experience traditions firsthand. Whether it's a local food festival, a cultural parade, or a traditional dance performance, these events offer a glimpse into the soul of a culture. Engage with the people you meet, ask questions, and savor the opportunity to learn something new. These experiences not only build cultural competence but also create memories that enrich your life. Engaging in cross-cultural dialogues and discussions is another powerful way to expand your understanding. Join forums or groups dedicated to cultural exchange, where people share their insights and experiences. These platforms encourage dialogue, fostering an environment where learning from one another is a natural outcome.

Reflection Section: Cultural Curiosity Journal

Consider starting a "Cultural Curiosity Journal." Document your experiences with different cultures, noting any new insights or realizations. Reflect on how these experiences have influenced your perspective and understanding. This practice encourages ongoing learning and appreciation for the rich tapestry of human culture.

By embracing cultural differences with sensitivity and openness, you enhance your communication skills and build bridges in an increasingly interconnected world. Each interaction becomes an opportunity to learn and grow, enriching your life and those you encounter.

7:3 POTLUCKS AND WORK EVENTS: WHAT TO BRING AND HOW TO BEHAVE

Potlucks are more than just a gathering of dishes; they celebrate community and shared experiences. Imagine a table laden with a colorful array of foods, each dish telling a story of the person who brought it. This communal nature is what makes potlucks so unique. They foster a sense of team spirit and inclusion, with each participant contributing to the feast. Potlucks offer a unique opportunity to share diverse culinary experiences, where you might taste a spicy curry from one colleague and a traditional lasagna from another. This diversity not only tantalizes the taste buds but also opens doors to conversations about culture and personal stories, bridging gaps beyond the workplace. Encouraging everyone to participate, from the cooking enthusiast to the novice, ensures a well-rounded event where everyone has a stake in the outcome.

Consider the group's dietary restrictions and preferences when selecting a dish to bring. In today's world, where gluten-free, vegan, and nut-free diets are typical, choosing a dish that accommodates various needs or is easy to adapt is considerate. Dishes that are easy to serve and share, like casseroles, salads, or finger foods, are ideal. They minimize the need for extra utensils and make it simple for guests to grab a portion without disrupting the event flow. Think about the logistics, too—will your dish need reheating, or can it be served cold? Planning these details ensures your contribution is both delicious and practical.

Serving and consuming food at these events requires etiquette to keep things pleasant. When serving yourself, be mindful of portion sizes. Taking a modest amount allows everyone to sample each dish and reduces the risk of running out of food. If you're first in line, leave enough for those who come after. When it comes to food preferences and allergies, sensitivity is key. If you know someone has an allergy, make sure your dish is clearly labeled or keep a list of ingredients handy. This simple act of consideration can prevent unwanted reactions and shows respect for the health and preferences of your colleagues.

Contributing positively to work events goes beyond the food you bring. Volunteering for setup and cleanup is a practical way to engage constructively. Arriving early to help with table arrangements or staying afterward to tidy up demonstrates teamwork and a willingness to support your peers. It's also an excellent way to socialize outside of your usual work interactions, allowing you to connect with colleagues you might not work closely with on a daily basis. Balancing socializing with professional conduct is another crucial element. While potlucks are a relaxed environment, maintaining professionalism is essential. Engage in light-hearted conversations and enjoy the atmosphere, but remain mindful of topics suitable for a work setting. Avoid discussing sensitive work matters unless you're in a private conversation, and steer clear of gossip or controversial subjects that might lead to discomfort.

Potlucks and work events offer a refreshing break from the everyday routine and provide a platform for colleagues to connect on a personal level. The shared experience of preparing, serving, and enjoying food together strengthens bonds and builds a sense of camaraderie. As you navigate these gatherings, remember that the focus is on community and collaboration, where every participant plays a part in creating a memorable and enjoyable occasion.

7:4 TIPPING IN SERVICE INDUSTRIES: WHY IT MATTERS

Picture yourself enjoying a delicious meal at your favorite local diner. The waiter was attentive, refilled your drink without asking, and even recommended the perfect dessert. As you finish, you consider how much to tip. Tipping is more than a mere financial transaction; it's a vital service industry component, intertwining economic necessity with social appreciation. For many service workers, tips are not just bonuses but essential supplements to often modest wages. In places where the minimum wage for tipped employees is lower than the standard, these earnings can significantly impact a worker's livelihood. By tipping, you acknowledge their effort and the quality service they provide, directly contributing to their income and wellbeing.

Knowing the appropriate amount can sometimes feel like navigating a maze when tipping. However, there are general guidelines that can simplify this process. In restaurants, cafes, and bars, a tip of 15-20% of the total bill is customary in the United States, reflecting gratitude for the service received. For delivery services, such as pizza or groceries, offering a tip of around 10% or a flat rate of $5 is a thoughtful gesture. Personal care services like haircuts or manicures usually warrant a 15-20% tip. These practices show appreciation and ensure that those who serve us are fairly compensated for their time and effort.

Understanding that tipping customs can vary significantly across the globe is crucial, especially if you enjoy traveling. In some countries, like Japan, tipping can be perceived as insulting, as service is considered part of the job and not something that needs additional reward. Conversely, in places like the United States and Canada, tipping is integral to the dining and service experience.

Europe offers a mixed bag, where a service charge is often included in the bill, but a small additional tip is appreciated. When abroad, adapting your tipping habits to align with local customs reflects cultural sensitivity and respect. Before you travel, a quick search or consulting a tipping guide can equip you with the knowledge to navigate these differences gracefully, ensuring you don't inadvertently offend or shortchange.

While tipping is essentially a personal decision, it's essential to consider the broader implications of your choices. Responsible and fair tipping reflects gratitude, respect, and support for the hardworking individuals who enhance your dining or service experience. When you receive exceptional service, consider tipping on the higher end of the scale. Acknowledging those who go above and beyond rewards them for their dedication and encourages them to maintain high standards in their work. On the other hand, neglecting to tip, especially in cultures where it is expected, can negatively impact the livelihood of those who rely on these earnings. It's worth reflecting on the message your tipping habits send and how they align with your values of fairness and appreciation.

In closing this chapter, remember that tipping is a small but significant gesture. It's a way to say "thank you" that goes beyond words, contributing to the fabric of social and economic interactions in everyday life. Mastering the nuances of tipping enhances your dining and service experiences and supports the individuals who make those experiences memorable. As we conclude this exploration of etiquette and cultural competence, consider how these principles apply to other facets of adult life, setting the stage for the next chapter.

CHAPTER 8

DIGITAL LITERACY AND ONLINE SAFETY

"In the digital age, your reputation is your most valuable asset."

— UNKNOWN

Consider this: you're sipping your morning coffee, scrolling through your favorite social media feed when a message claims you've won a prize. All you need to do is click the link. Seems harmless, right? But in today's digital age, this could be a trap set by cybercriminals. The digital world offers endless opportunities, yet it also comes with risks that you must navigate wisely. Cybersecurity has become a crucial part of our everyday lives, especially with the rise in digital activity. According to the Microsoft Digital Defense Report 2023, cyber threats are not just growing, they are proliferating at an alarming rate, with identity theft and data breaches becoming increasingly common. The Federal Trade Commission received 5.7 million reports of identity theft and fraud in 2021 alone, resulting in over $5.8 billion in losses. These statistics reflect the pervasive nature of cybersecurity threats and the importance of protecting your personal and financial information.

8:1 UNDERSTANDING CYBERSECURITY AND PROTECTING YOUR DATA

Understanding the spectrum of cybersecurity threats is the first step in safeguarding your digital life. Phishing, for instance, is a common tactic where cybercriminals pose as legitimate entities to steal sensitive information. They might send emails or messages that look authentic, prompting you to click on malicious links. Malware, another prevalent threat, refers to software designed to damage or gain unauthorized access to your computer. Such threats can lead to significant data loss, financial fraud, and even identity theft. Recognizing these dangers is essential for taking proactive measures to protect yourself online.

To shield your personal information, start with strong, unique passwords. Avoid using easily guessable passwords like "123456" or "password." Instead, create complex ones with a mix of letters, numbers, and symbols, such as "P@ssword123!" or "Tru3Lov3&H@ppin3ss". Password managers can help you keep track of your credentials without remembering each one. Two-factor authentication adds an extra layer of security by requiring a second verification form—such as a text message or app notification—before accessing your account. This step makes it significantly harder for unauthorized users to gain control.

Utilizing software and tools enhances your security further. Antivirus and anti-malware programs are your first line of defense against malicious software. Regularly updating these programs ensures they can detect the latest threats. Similarly, a Virtual Private Network (VPN) can protect your internet connection, especially on public Wi-Fi. A VPN encrypts your data, making it difficult for hackers to intercept your information. This tool is handy when accessing the internet from cafes, airports, or public spots where the network is shared among many users.

Despite common myths, no system is entirely immune to cyber threats. A prevalent misconception is that Macs are invulnerable to viruses. While Macs have built-in security features, they are not impervious to malware. Cybercriminals design threats for all operating systems, and complacency can lead to vulnerabilities. Another false belief is that browsing on public Wi-Fi with HTTPS is always safe. Although HTTPS encrypts data between your browser and the website, it doesn't protect against all types of cyber attacks. Hackers can still exploit unsecured networks to access your device and data.

Interactive Element: Cybersecurity Self-Assessment

Take a moment to evaluate your digital security practices. Consider the strength of your passwords, your use of two-factor authentication, and whether you have up-to-date antivirus software. Reflect on your habits when using public Wi-Fi and make a plan to address any vulnerabilities. This self-assessment is crucial for identifying areas where you can bolster your defenses and ensure your online safety.

In the digital realm, safeguarding your information is as crucial as locking your front door at night. By understanding cybersecurity threats and implementing protective measures, you can confidently navigate the online world. Remember, staying informed and proactive about your digital habits is not just the key to staying safe, it's the key to feeling empowered in the digital age.

8:2 DIGITAL ETIQUETTE IN PROFESSIONAL AND PERSONAL SETTINGS

Imagine sending a quick email to your boss to clarify a minor detail. Still, in your haste, you forget to correctly add a greeting or sign off. The message comes across as abrupt, perhaps even rude, and suddenly, a simple oversight has altered the tone of your professional relationship. This is where digital etiquette steps in. Digital etiquette, or netiquette, is not just about maintaining professionalism and respect in all online interactions, it's about preserving the integrity of your professional relationships. In today's world, where much of our communication occurs digitally, understanding and practicing good etiquette is crucial. Poor digital etiquette can result in misunderstandings or even damage your reputation. For instance, typing in all caps may seem like you're shouting, while neglecting to proofread can lead to errors that reflect poorly on your attention to detail. The tone of your emails and messages plays a critical role, as the absence of vocal inflection can lead to misinterpretations. Being mindful of how your words might be perceived can prevent unnecessary conflicts or confusion.

Mastering digital etiquette across various platforms requires adapting your communication style to fit the context. In professional settings, email etiquette is paramount. Always start with a courteous greeting and conclude with a respectful closing. Use a clear subject line that succinctly summarizes the email's purpose. Keep your message concise and to the point, but provide enough detail to avoid back-and-forth exchanges. For social media, remember that your posts reflect your personal brand. Adjust your privacy settings to control who can see your content, and be mindful of the information you share publicly. Avoid posting in the heat of the moment; instead, take a moment to reflect on whether your words could be misinterpreted or cause harm. It's important to remember that everything you do online leaves a 'digital footprint', a trail of data that you leave behind. This can be a positive or negative reflection of your online behavior. Maintaining this awareness ensures that your digital footprint remains positive and professional.

Digital communication can significantly impact both personal and professional relationships. The way you interact online can strengthen connections or create rifts. When faced with negative comments or feedback, responding with grace is key. For instance, if someone criticizes your work, you could acknowledge their feedback, thank them for taking the time to share their thoughts, and explain how you plan to address their concerns. Avoid reacting impulsively, as this can escalate the situation. Instead, acknowledge the comment respectfully and, if appropriate, offer a constructive response. This approach demonstrates maturity and the ability to handle criticism effectively. Balancing personal and professional personas online is also crucial. While it's essential to be authentic, consider your posts' potential reach and impact. What you share with friends might not be suitable for colleagues or professional contacts. Striking this balance ensures your online presence reflects the multifaceted aspects of your personality without crossing boundaries.

Mindfulness in digital interactions promotes positive communication and helps prevent unintended consequences. Before posting or commenting, consider the potential impact of your words. Reflect on whether your message aligns with your values and respects others' perspectives. Cultural and contextual differences should also be taken into account. What might be acceptable in one culture could be offensive in another. By being aware of these nuances, you can engage in more inclusive and respectful communication. Digital interactions, while convenient, have real-world repercussions. A careless comment can damage relationships or tarnish your reputation. Practicing mindfulness encourages thoughtful engagement and fosters a more positive online environment.

In the digital age, understanding and applying digital etiquette is essential for maintaining healthy relationships and a professional image. Whether emailing a potential employer, posting on social media, or texting a friend, respect, clarity, and mindfulness should guide your interactions. By doing so, you enhance your communication skills and build a reputation for being considerate and reliable in both personal and professional contexts. This awareness brings about a more harmonious digital landscape, where interactions are guided by empathy and understanding, allowing you to navigate the complexities of digital communication with confidence and poise.

8:3 MANAGING YOUR DIGITAL FOOTPRINT

Picture this: every photo you post, every comment you drop, and every blog you write contributes to a digital footprint. It's like leaving a trail of breadcrumbs across the internet, marking your path for all to see. Unlike footprints in the sand that the tide washes away, your digital footprint can be surprisingly permanent. Search engines can pull up posts from years ago, and what you thought was a throwaway comment could resurface at the most inconvenient time, like during a job application process. Is a common practice for employers to conduct online checks, not just relying on your resume or interview. In fact, they might judge your suitability based on the persona they find online. This can work for you or against you. A well-groomed digital presence can showcase your professionalism and creativity, while a careless footprint might cost you an opportunity.

Managing your digital footprint requires intentionality. First, regularly audit your online profiles and content. This means going through your social media, blogs, and other platforms where you have a presence. Look at what's public and consider its impact. Is there an old tweet that no longer aligns with your values or a photo that doesn't reflect your current self? Removing outdated or inappropriate posts is crucial. It's like spring cleaning for your online life. This isn't about erasing your past but curating a present that accurately represents who you are now. Check privacy settings frequently. Platforms update these settings, sometimes changing what's visible to the public. Ensure your profiles share only what you're comfortable with the world seeing.

Privacy settings are your allies when controlling personal information. Social media platforms provide various options to manage who can see your content. You can often adjust these settings to limit visibility to friends or specific groups, reducing the risk of unwanted eyes on your personal life. Be cautious about third-party apps that request access to your data. Limiting data sharing with these apps protects your information from being sold or misused. Many apps offer a "permissions" section where you can see what data they access. Review these regularly and revoke permissions for apps you no longer use. This level of vigilance helps maintain control over your digital footprint and keeps your personal information safe from prying eyes.

A professional image online can be a powerful tool. Consistency across platforms is key to maintaining a coherent digital identity. This doesn't mean you can't have fun or show your personality.

Still, considering how your posts might be perceived by different audiences. Engaging with industry-related content can enhance your online presence. Share articles, comment on posts, and participate in discussions related to your field. This portrays you as knowledgeable and engaged and helps build connections with others in your industry. It's about balancing personal expression and professional polish, ensuring your digital footprint supports your goals and aspirations.

Checklist: Curating Your Digital Presence

1. **Audit Online Profiles:** Regularly review content on all your platforms. Remove anything outdated or misaligned with your current values.
2. **Adjust Privacy Settings:** Revisit privacy options on social media to control who sees your information and limit data sharing with third-party apps.
3. **Engage Professionally:** Share and comment on industry-related content. Join discussions to highlight your expertise and interest.
4. **Maintain Consistency:** Ensure your online image matches your professional aspirations across different platforms.

Following this checklist, you actively shape a digital footprint that reflects your true self and supports your professional and personal aspirations.

8:4 ONLINE NETWORKING AND PROFESSIONAL BRANDING

In today's digital landscape, building an online network is more than sending friend requests or connecting on social media. It's about creating a web of relationships that can open doors, provide mentorship, and even lead to unexpected career opportunities. Think of it as expanding your circle in a way that lets you tap into a wealth of knowledge and experiences. Connecting with industry professionals through platforms like LinkedIn lets you gain insights into your field, discover new trends, and even find job leads. Expanding your influence through digital platforms allows you to showcase your skills and ideas to a broader audience, potentially attracting opportunities you hadn't considered.

Crafting and maintaining a professional online brand requires intention and consistency. Your online presence is like a digital resume that speaks loudly about your professionalism and expertise. Start by creating a compelling LinkedIn profile. Ensure your profile picture is professional, and your headline reflects your current or desired role. Use the summary section to tell your story—highlight your achievements, skills, and career goals in an engaging and authentic way. Sharing your expertise through blogs or online articles is another powerful way to build your brand. Write about topics you are passionate about or have insight into. This establishes you as a thought leader in your field and helps others see the value you bring to the table.

Social media plays a crucial role in professional networking. It's a tool that, when used wisely, can enhance your career prospects significantly. Engage with professional groups and discussions online. Participating in industry-specific forums or comment sections allows you to share views and learn from others.

Following and interacting with industry leaders can also be beneficial. Comment on their posts, share their work, and contribute to the conversations they start. This not only puts you on their radar but can also lead to more meaningful interactions down the line. Remember, the goal is to build genuine relationships, not just to network for networking's sake.

Balancing your personal and professional online identities is essential to presenting a cohesive yet authentic self. While it's natural to want to share aspects of your personal life online, it's necessary to consider how this might intersect with your professional image. One strategy is to separate personal and professional accounts. Use one set of social media accounts to connect with friends and family while maintaining another for professional interactions. This allows you to express yourself freely in your personal life while keeping your professional persona polished and consistent. Managing cross-platform consistency is also critical. Ensure that your message and branding remain uniform across different networks. This cohesiveness strengthens your online presence, making it clear to anyone who encounters you what you stand for and what you can offer.

As we wrap up this chapter on digital literacy and online safety, remember that your online presence is a powerful tool. By understanding cybersecurity, practicing good digital etiquette, managing your digital footprint, and developing your professional brand, you're not just protecting yourself; you're positioning yourself for success. In the next chapter, we'll explore personal safety and preparedness, equipping you with the knowledge to stay safe in the real world just as you do online.

CHAPTER 9
PERSONAL SAFETY AND PREPAREDNESS

"Safety doesn't happen by accident."

— UNKNOWN

Imagine you're at a bustling café, enjoying a latte and a good book when someone nearby suddenly collapses. The room freezes, eyes wide, breaths held, and time seems to stop for a moment. This scenario highlights the unpredictability of emergencies and the crucial need for you to be prepared. Knowing basic first aid can make the difference between panic and action in such moments. It's not just about being a good Samaritan; it's about having the confidence to step in and help when someone needs it most. Whether dealing with a minor scrape or a more serious situation, being equipped with fundamental first aid skills can empower you to act decisively and effectively, giving you a sense of control in uncertain situations. Let's dive into the essential techniques you should know.

9:1 BASIC FIRST AID SKILLS EVERYONE SHOULD KNOW

When treating cuts and scrapes, the first step is cleaning the wound to prevent infection. Rinse the cut under running water and gently wash around it with soap. If there's debris, use tweezers sterilized with rubbing alcohol to remove it carefully. Once clean, apply an antibiotic ointment to keep bacteria at bay, then cover the wound with a sterile bandage. Change the bandage daily or whenever it gets wet or dirty. This simple process not only protects the wound but also promotes faster healing. The R.I.C.E. method —Rest, Ice, Compression, Elevation—comes into play for sprains and strains. Rest the injured area to prevent further damage, apply ice packs to reduce swelling, wrap it with a compression bandage for support, and elevate it above heart level to minimize puffiness. These steps can alleviate pain and speed up recovery, allowing you to return to your routine sooner.

Knowing CPR (Cardiopulmonary Resuscitation) can be lifesaving, especially in situations where someone is unresponsive and not breathing. Begin by checking the scene to ensure safety, then approach the person, calling out and tapping their shoulder to check for responsiveness. If there's no response, call emergency services immediately. Place the person on their back on a firm surface and kneel beside them. Open their airway by tilting their head back slightly and lifting their chin. Check for breathing by placing your ear near your mouth and looking for chest movement. If they aren't breathing, start chest compressions. Place the heel of one hand on the center of their chest, right between the nipples, and place your other hand on top. Push hard and fast, about 100 to 120 compressions per minute, allowing the chest to rise fully between compressions. If you're trained, give two rescue breaths after every 30 compressions. Pinch the person's nose shut, seal your mouth over theirs, and blow until you see their chest rise. Continue this cycle until help arrives or the person starts breathing.

Choking is another emergency where swift action is crucial. For adults, the Heimlich maneuver is the go-to technique. Stand behind the person, wrap your arms around their waist, and make a fist with one hand. Place the thumb side of your fist above their navel, grasp it with your other hand, and perform quick upward thrusts until the object is expelled. For infants, lay them face down along your forearm, supporting their head and neck. Deliver five back blows between the shoulder blades with the heel of your hand, then turn them over and give five chest thrusts using two fingers on the center of the chest. For pregnant individuals, place your hands higher, at the base of the breastbone, and perform the Heimlich maneuver as usual.

Sometimes, despite your best efforts, a situation requires professional medical assistance. Recognizing when to call for help is as vital as administering first aid. Signs of shock—such as pale skin, rapid breathing, or confusion—indicate a serious issue that warrants immediate attention. Similarly, severe bleeding that doesn't stop with direct pressure or any situation where the person remains unresponsive after CPR calls for urgent medical intervention. Understanding the limits of first aid ensures you don't take on more than you can safely handle, keeping you and the victim safe until professionals arrive.

Interactive Element: First Aid Practice Checklist

Create a "First Aid Practice Checklist" to reinforce your skills. This checklist should include practicing CPR compressions on a dummy, simulating the Heimlich maneuver, and applying bandages correctly. Regular practice is not just a suggestion, it's a responsibility. It helps keep your skills sharp, ensuring you're ready to respond in an emergency. It's a commitment to yourself and to those around you that you take their safety seriously.

Being prepared to handle emergencies with basic first aid skills not only boosts your confidence but also equips you to make a real difference when it matters most. Whether a simple cut or a more complex scenario, your knowledge and readiness can provide comfort and aid when others need it most. The relief you can bring to a person in distress, the comfort you can provide to a worried family member, these are the moments that make your preparedness truly valuable.

9.2 CREATING A HOME EMERGENCY PREPAREDNESS PLAN

Picture this: you're at home, the sky darkens outside, and the news alert flashes across your screen, warning of an impending storm. There's a moment of panic—what do you do now? Being prepared for emergencies, whether natural or not, can alleviate this anxiety. The first step in creating a robust emergency preparedness plan is understanding the risks specific to your area. For instance, hurricanes might be your primary concern if you live in a coastal region. In contrast, those in the Midwest might focus more on tornadoes. Researching local hazards helps tailor your plan, ensuring you anticipate the most likely scenarios.

Once you identify potential threats, it's time to develop a comprehensive emergency plan. Start by outlining an evacuation route. Consider various scenarios to determine the safest paths out of your home and neighborhood. Having multiple exits mapped out is wise so you're prepared if your primary route becomes inaccessible. Also, meeting points should be established where family or roommates can regroup if separated. Choose locations that are familiar and easily accessible, like a nearby park or a friend's house. Communication is key during emergencies, so designate emergency contacts outside your immediate area who can act as liaisons. Ensure everyone knows how to reach these contacts through phone, email, or social media.

An emergency kit is a cornerstone of preparedness, acting as a lifeline when regular resources become unavailable. Stock it with non-perishable food and water supplies for at least three days. Think canned goods, granola bars, and bottled water. Flashlights with extra batteries are crucial for power outages, providing much-needed light and comfort in dark times. A first aid kit is indispensable, equipped with bandages, antiseptic wipes, and necessary medications. Personalize your kit to include items specific to your household's needs, such as pet food, baby supplies, or prescription medications. Keep this kit in an easily accessible spot, ready to grab at a moment's notice.

Regularly reviewing and practicing your emergency plan keeps it fresh and compelling. Conduct drills with family or roommates, simulating scenarios to ensure everyone knows their roles and responsibilities. This practice reinforces the plan and fosters a sense of calm and readiness. Review your emergency supplies, check expiry dates on food and medicine, and replenish items as needed. Life changes, so update the plan to reflect new family members, pets, or living arrangements.

Interactive Element: Emergency Preparedness Checklist

Create an "Emergency Preparedness Checklist" to ensure your plan covers all bases. Include sections for assessing risks, developing evacuation routes, assembling an emergency kit, and scheduling practice drills. This checklist serves as a tangible reminder to keep your preparedness efforts on track and up to date.

Being proactive in emergency preparedness equips you with the tools and confidence to face uncertainties head-on. It's about creating a security shield for you and your loved ones, knowing that whatever the storm brings, you're ready to weather it with resilience and composure.

9.3 UNDERSTANDING AND USING FIRE SAFETY EQUIPMENT

Picture yourself in your cozy living room, enjoying a quiet evening with a scented candle flickering gently on the table. It's a calm scene, yet it can quickly turn into a dangerous situation without proper precautions. Fire safety equipment is your first line of defense against such risks, ensuring that your home remains a safe haven. Smoke detectors and carbon monoxide detectors are crucial tools in this arsenal. Smoke detectors alert you to smoke, warning you early of a possible fire. Install them on every level of your home, especially near sleeping areas, to maximize their effectiveness.

On the other hand, carbon monoxide detectors detect the colorless, odorless gas that can be deadly if undetected. Place these near bedrooms and fuel-burning appliances. Together, these devices form the backbone of your fire safety strategy, giving you a vital head start in an emergency.

Fire extinguishers are indispensable for tackling small fires before they escalate. They come in different classifications—A, B, and C—each designed for specific types of fires. Class A extinguishers are effective against ordinary combustibles like wood and paper. Class B extinguishers are suited for flammable liquids such as grease and gasoline. Class C extinguishers target electrical fires. Understanding these classifications helps you choose the right extinguisher for your home. It's wise to have one on each floor, particularly in the kitchen and garage, where fires are more likely to start. Storing them in an easily accessible location ensures you can act swiftly if a fire breaks out, potentially saving your property and lives.

Proper installation and maintenance of fire safety devices are crucial to their effectiveness. Smoke detectors should be tested monthly to ensure they're functioning correctly. Press the test button; you're good to go if the alarm sounds. If not, replace the batteries immediately. Most detectors have a lifespan of about ten years, so mark your calendar for a replacement. Fire extinguishers also require regular checks. Inspect the pressure gauge monthly to ensure it's in the green zone, indicating it's ready for use. If the extinguisher has been used, even partially, replace or recharge it promptly. Regular maintenance ensures your fire safety equipment is always ready to protect you when needed.

Knowing how to use a fire extinguisher can make all the difference in an emergency. The PASS technique—Pull, Aim, Squeeze, Sweep—provides a straightforward method. Start by pulling the pin to break the tamper seal. Aim the nozzle at the base of the fire, as this is where the fuel source lies. Squeeze the handle to release the extinguishing agent, and sweep the nozzle from side to side until the fire is out. It's essential to stand about eight feet away from the fire, moving closer as the flames subside. Always keep your back to an exit, ensuring a clear escape route if the fire grows beyond control. Familiarizing yourself with these steps prepares you to act confidently and effectively when seconds count.

Prevention is always better than reaction; minimizing fire risks in your home is essential. Candles should never be left unattended. Use sturdy holders and avoid flammable materials like curtains or paper. Consider using flameless LED candles for ambiance without the risk. Electrical appliances also pose fire hazards if misused. Avoid overloading outlets and regularly check cords for fraying or damage. Unplug appliances when not in use to prevent overheating. Flammable materials, such as cleaning products or paints, should be stored in a cool, dry place away from heat sources. Keeping these items organized reduces the risk of accidental ignition.

Creating a fire-safe environment involves awareness and routine. Regularly review your home for potential hazards and address them promptly. Encourage everyone in your household to participate in fire safety practices, reinforcing the importance of vigilance. By integrating these habits into your daily life, you cultivate a culture of safety that protects you and your loved ones from the unexpected.

9.4 STAYING SAFE IN NEW ENVIRONMENTS

Imagine stepping off a bus in a city you've never visited before. The streets are unfamiliar, and the hustle and bustle of daily life are both exciting and overwhelming. In these moments, assessing your surroundings for safety becomes crucial. Start by identifying exits and escape routes. Whether in a café or a shopping mall, make it a habit to look for exit signs and paths that lead to safety. This simple act can prepare you for an emergency, like a fire or a sudden evacuation. Observe the behavior of those around you, too. People often give subtle cues about an area's safety, such as if they notice a crowd gathering or people moving quickly in one direction. In that case, it might indicate a situation you must know.

When traveling or exploring new places, safeguarding your belongings can prevent a carefree adventure from turning into a stressful ordeal. Keep valuables secure and out of sight. Use a money belt or a hidden pouch for your passport and money, and avoid flashing expensive gadgets in crowded places. Opt for cross-body bags that you can keep close to your body, making it harder for pickpockets to target you. Additionally, choose reputable transportation options. Research local taxi services or use ride-sharing apps with good reviews. Public transport can be safe, but remain cautious, especially when crowded. Standing near the driver or in well-lit areas can provide security.

Handling unexpected situations calmly is a skill that can be developed with practice. Trust your instincts. If something feels off, it usually is. Don't hesitate to remove yourself from an uncomfortable situation, whether leaving a party early or walking away from a suspicious vendor. Seek help from authorities or locals if you find yourself in a bind. Police officers, security personnel, and shopkeepers can offer guidance and assistance. Learning a few basic phrases in the local language can also be incredibly helpful. "Help," "police," and "emergency" are good words to know, as they can facilitate communication in critical moments.

Promoting awareness and self-defense skills boosts your confidence and preparedness in unfamiliar settings. Self-defense classes teach techniques to protect yourself physically and enhance your awareness of your surroundings. They instill a sense of readiness, empowering you to handle potential threats. Staying aware of your environment is key. Avoid distractions like excessive phone use when walking in unfamiliar areas. Instead, stay alert and attentive to what's happening around you. This vigilance helps you enjoy your surroundings more fully and prepares you to react quickly if needed.

Interactive Element: Personal Safety Reflection Exercise

Set aside time for a "Personal Safety Reflection Exercise." Consider recent experiences in new environments and evaluate your responses. Were you aware of exits? Did you feel secure with your belongings? Reflecting on these situations helps reinforce positive habits and identify areas for improvement.

Navigating new environments with an eye toward safety doesn't have to be daunting. With awareness and preparation, you can confidently explore, knowing you're equipped to handle whatever comes your way. Whether it's a bustling urban area or a quiet rural town, these skills are your allies in making the most of your adventures while keeping safety at the forefront.

As we conclude this chapter on personal safety and preparedness, remember that these skills protect you and empower you to live confidently. Being prepared makes all the difference whether you're at home or exploring new horizons. In the next chapter, we'll explore how to apply this same confidence and preparedness to manage your finances, ensuring you're ready to handle the responsibilities of financial independence.

CHAPTER 10
PERSONAL GROWTH AND LIFE PLANNING

"Your life does not get better by chance; it gets better by change."

— JIM ROHN

Imagine you are standing at the start of a new year, brimming with the excitement of endless possibilities. You have a fresh planner ready to fill it with dreams and ambitions. Yet, without clear goals, these dreams might remain just that—dreams. Setting achievable goals is like building a roadmap for your life, providing direction and motivation to pursue your aspirations. It's about giving shape to your ambitions and transforming them into tangible milestones, empowering you to take control of your life and feel confident in your journey.

10:1 SETTING ACHIEVABLE GOALS AND TRACKING PROGRESS

Differentiating between short-term and long-term goals is essential. Short-term goals often pave the way for long-term success. They could be as simple as saving a certain amount each month or completing a certification course. Long-term goals include career advancement or buying a home. The SMART criteria—Specific, Measurable, Achievable, Relevant, and Time-bound—are vital in goal-setting (Source 1). For instance, rather than saying, "I want to save money," a SMART goal would be, "I will save $500 in three months by setting aside $50 weekly." This method turns vague intentions into clear, actionable plans.

Breaking down large goals into manageable steps can prevent overwhelm and foster progress. Creating actionable to-do lists is a practical strategy. By writing down tasks and prioritizing them based on urgency and importance, you gain clarity on what needs immediate attention and what can wait. Tackling one task at a time can create a sense of accomplishment and build momentum. It's the small, consistent steps that eventually lead to significant achievements. This approach makes the process less intimidating and more achievable, providing a sense of relief and ease in your journey.

Tracking progress is crucial to staying on course and making necessary adjustments. Digital tools like Trello or Todoist can be invaluable. They allow you to organize tasks visually, set deadlines, and track accomplishments. These tools can be reminders and motivators, showing you how far you've come and what lies ahead. Maintaining a progress journal is another effective technique. It provides a space to reflect on your journey, document challenges and victories, and gain insights into your growth.

Regularly reviewing your journal can offer perspective and inspire perseverance, leaving you feeling motivated and inspired by your own progress.

Flexibility in goal-setting is as important as the goals themselves. Life is unpredictable, and circumstances can change, requiring you to adapt your plans. Reviewing goals quarterly allows you to assess their relevance and feasibility. During these reviews, consider any new insights or changes in your situation. A goal that seemed vital a few months ago no longer aligns with your current priorities. Embracing this flexibility ensures that your goals continue to serve your best interests. Adjusting goals doesn't mean failure; it signifies growth and self-awareness.

Reflection Section: Goal-Setting Journal Prompt

Create a dedicated section in your journal for goal-setting reflections. Each week, jot down what you've accomplished, what challenged you, and what you learned. Reflect on how your goals align with your current values and priorities. This practice keeps you accountable and deepens your understanding of your personal growth journey.

10:2 DEVELOPING A PERSONAL GROWTH MINDSET

Imagine seeing a roadblock as a dead end versus a stepping stone. This distinction captures the essence of a growth mindset versus a fixed mindset. A growth mindset, a concept introduced by psychologist Carol Dweck, is about believing in your potential for self-improvement. It's the understanding that abilities and intelligence can be developed through dedication and effort. This perspective transforms challenges into opportunities for learning rather than insurmountable obstacles. In contrast, a fixed mindset holds that talents and intelligence are static traits, leading to a desire to constantly prove oneself. Embracing a growth mindset can significantly enhance personal and professional development, encouraging resilience and adaptability in adversity (Source 2).

Cultivating a growth mindset involves conscious effort and practical strategies. Start by practicing self-affirmation and positive self-talk. These techniques reinforce the belief that you are capable of growth and change. Replace thoughts like "I can't do this" with "I can learn how to do this." Seeking feedback and constructive criticism is another powerful way to nurture growth. Instead of viewing criticism as a personal attack, see it as valuable insight into areas for improvement. Feedback can catalyze development, helping you identify strengths and weaknesses you might not have seen on your own. Embracing input with an open mind can accelerate your growth journey, transforming perceived failures into valuable lessons.

However, adopting a growth mindset is not without its challenges. Mental blocks like fear of failure and perfectionist tendencies can impede progress. The fear of failure often stems from a fixed mindset, where mistakes are seen as reflections of one's abilities. To overcome this, reframe failure as a part of the learning process —each misstep is simply a lesson in disguise. Similarly, perfectionism can be paralyzing, preventing you from starting or completing tasks for fear of imperfection. Challenge this by setting realistic standards and acknowledging that growth is gradual. Understanding that perfection is unattainable allows you to focus on progress rather than flawlessness.

The impact of a growth mindset extends far beyond personal development. It enhances resilience, enabling you to face setbacks with determination rather than defeat. When you believe in your capacity to grow, challenges become less daunting, and persistence becomes second nature. Furthermore, a growth-oriented perspective fosters creativity and problem-solving skills. By viewing problems as puzzles to be solved rather than insurmountable barriers, you open yourself to innovative solutions and new approaches. Embracing a growth mindset can transform how you approach life and work, enabling you to thrive in an ever-changing world.

10:3 PLANNING FOR MAJOR LIFE CHANGES AND TRANSITIONS

Picture yourself standing at the crossroads of life, diploma in hand, ready to step into the workforce. It's an exciting yet daunting moment of anticipation and uncertainty. Navigating this transition with confidence begins with preparation. Graduating and entering the workforce requires more than just a polished resume. It involves understanding the new landscape, setting clear expectations, and being open to learning. Embrace the opportunity to grow, even if it means starting at the bottom. Relocating to a new city or country adds another layer of complexity. It's not just about packing boxes; it's about embracing a new environment, culture, and community. Research the area, understand the local norms, and plan your move meticulously to ensure a smoother transition.

The emotional and psychological aspects of change are often underestimated. Change can stir anxiety, uncertainty, and even fear. It's natural to feel overwhelmed by the unknown. Coping with these emotions involves acknowledging them rather than pushing them aside. Establishing a support system can provide the emotional stability needed during such times. Friends, family, or even professional networks offer invaluable support, helping you navigate the emotional rollercoaster with greater resilience. They can remind you that you're not alone, providing a safe space to express your feelings and seek advice. Building connections in your new environment can also help ease the transition, creating a sense of belonging and community.

Setting realistic expectations is key to managing transitions effectively. Life rarely goes according to plan, and preparing for potential challenges can soften the blow of unexpected hurdles. Approach changes with a balanced outlook, recognizing that setbacks are not failures but opportunities for growth. Flexibility and adaptability are your allies. Plans may need to shift, and that's okay. The ability to pivot and adjust your course ensures you're not derailed by unforeseen circumstances. Whether it's a job that didn't turn out as expected or a city that feels different from what you imagined, maintaining an open mind allows you to find joy and fulfillment in the unexpected.

Creating a transition action plan can transform chaos into clarity. Start by setting timelines and milestones to keep track of progress. These serve as guideposts, helping you measure your achievements and adjust your path. Identify resources and support networks that can assist you along the way. Whether it's a mentor who can offer career advice or online communities that share your interests, these networks provide guidance and encouragement. A structured approach reduces stress and empowers you to take control of your transitions, turning potential obstacles into stepping stones toward personal and professional growth.

10:4 BUILDING A SUPPORTIVE NETWORK AND LEARNING COMMUNITY

Imagine stepping into a room where everyone radiates positivity and encouragement. Surrounding yourself with such influences can profoundly impact your personal growth. A strong network acts as a catalyst for development, offering guidance and motivation when you need it most. Building relationships with mentors and peers who share your ambitions can open doors to new perspectives and opportunities. With their wealth of experience, mentors provide valuable insights and advice, helping you navigate challenges confidently. Peers, conversely, can offer camaraderie and support, making pursuing your goals a shared adventure rather than a solitary journey. Engaging in community or interest groups further enriches your experience, connecting you with like-minded individuals who inspire and challenge you to reach new heights.

Connecting with supportive individuals requires intentional effort and thoughtful engagement. Attending networking events and seminars is an excellent way to meet people who share your interests and aspirations. These gatherings provide a relaxed environment to exchange ideas and build meaningful connections. Social media also plays a crucial role in expanding your network. Platforms like LinkedIn offer a space to engage professionally, allowing you to connect with industry leaders and potential mentors. You establish yourself as a thoughtful and engaged community member by actively participating in discussions and contributing valuable insights. Remember, building a network is not about quantity but quality. Focus on developing genuine relationships with individuals who resonate with your values and goals.

Sustaining meaningful connections over time requires nurturing and effort. Regular check-ins demonstrate your interest in maintaining the relationship, whether through a quick message or a coffee catch-up. Offering assistance and value to others can also strengthen bonds. Whether sharing an article that might interest them or introducing them to someone in your network, these small gestures build goodwill and reciprocity. As you nurture these relationships, you'll find that your network becomes a source of encouragement and support, enriching your personal and professional life.

Lifelong learning communities offer an invaluable platform for continuous education and knowledge sharing. Joining online forums and workshops keeps you abreast of the latest developments in your field and expands your network. These spaces encourage collaboration and the exchange of ideas, fostering a culture of learning and growth. Participating in book clubs or study groups is another way to engage with others who share your interests. These communities provide a space for discussion and reflection, deepening your understanding of various topics. Embracing opportunities for lifelong learning ensures that you remain curious and adaptable, ready to tackle new challenges and seize new opportunities as they arise.

10:5 EMBRACING LIFE'S CHALLENGES WITH RESILIENCE

Life is full of unexpected twists and turns, and resilience is the quality that helps you navigate through them. At its core, resilience is the ability to bounce back from setbacks and continue moving forward. It's about finding your footing after a stumble and using your inner strength to rise again. Identifying personal strengths and resources is crucial in building resilience. These strengths could be anything from creativity to adaptability, and they act as anchors during turbulent times. When you focus on what you can do rather than what you can't, you cultivate a positive outlook, even when faced with challenges.

To enhance your resilience, begin by developing problem-solving skills. This involves approaching difficulties with a solution-oriented mindset, evaluating options, and making informed decisions. Practicing mindfulness can also play a significant role in building resilience. Techniques like deep breathing and meditation help manage stress, allowing you to remain calm and composed. Stress management is not just about reducing stressors but also about enhancing your capacity to cope with them. Integrating these practices into your daily routine creates a mental toolkit that supports you in times of adversity.

Self-care is another cornerstone of resilience. It involves taking deliberate actions to nurture your physical and emotional wellbeing. Establishing healthy routines can make a significant difference. This might include regular exercise, balanced nutrition, and ensuring you get enough sleep. Prioritizing rest and relaxation is equally important. In a world that often glorifies busyness, taking time to recharge is crucial. During these moments of rest, your body and mind can recover, preparing you to face new challenges with renewed energy.

Learning from adversity is one of the most potent aspects of resilience. Setbacks offer invaluable lessons that can lead to personal growth. Reflecting on past experiences helps you understand what worked and what didn't and how to apply these insights to future situations. Every challenge you overcome adds to your reservoir of wisdom, making you better equipped for the next one. Instead of viewing failures as final, see them as stepping stones to more significant achievements. This mindset transforms difficulties into opportunities for learning and development, enriching your life unexpectedly.

Interactive Element: Resilience Reflection Exercise

Take a moment to reflect on a recent challenge you faced. Write down what happened, how you responded, and what you learned from the experience. Consider how you can apply these insights to future challenges. This exercise helps you process your experiences and strengthens your ability to bounce back from adversity.

10:6 CREATING A BALANCED LIFE: WORK, PLAY, AND PERSONAL FULFILLMENT

Imagine waking up daily with purpose, knowing you have the time and energy to dedicate to work, personal interests, and relationships. This harmony is what life balance is all about. It's an ongoing process involving juggling various life aspects to promote overall wellbeing. At its core, achieving balance requires defining personal values and priorities. Identifying what truly matters to you—career success, family, health, or creativity—can guide your decisions and actions. Recognizing signs of imbalance, like chronic stress or neglect of personal relationships, is crucial. These signals often indicate a need to reassess your commitments and adjust to restore equilibrium.

Practical strategies are key to achieving a harmonious balance. Scheduling regular breaks and leisure activities is one such strategy. Short breaks throughout the day can refresh your mind and improve productivity. At the same time, more extended leisure activities—like a weekend hike or a creative class—can rejuvenate your spirit. Establishing boundaries between work and personal life is equally important. This might involve setting specific work hours and sticking to them or designating certain areas of your home as work-free zones. By clearly separating these spheres, you create space for relaxation and personal pursuits, preventing burnout and fostering fulfillment.

Pursuing hobbies and interests plays a vital role in personal fulfillment. These activities offer a chance to explore creative outlets and develop new skills, adding richness and diversity to your life. Whether painting, playing an instrument, or learning a new language, engaging in such pursuits can boost happiness and reduce stress. Sports and outdoor activities also contribute to well-being, offering physical benefits alongside mental relaxation. Joining a local team or running in the park can provide a sense of achievement and community, enhancing your overall quality of life.

Self-reflection is essential in maintaining balance. Regularly assessing your life allows you to ensure that your actions align with your personal goals and values. Life audits involve examining various aspects of your life—work, relationships, health—and evaluating their current state. This process can reveal areas needing attention or adjustment. Adjusting commitments and responsibilities as needed is part of this ongoing reflection. Perhaps a hobby has become less fulfilling, or a work project demands more time than anticipated. Being willing to make changes in response to these reflections ensures that your life remains aligned with your evolving priorities.

Interactive Element: Life Balance Checklist

Create a "Life Balance Checklist" to assess your current balance. Include categories like work hours, leisure activities, and time spent with loved ones. Regularly review this checklist to identify areas for improvement. This tool can guide you in making intentional adjustments to enhance your wellbeing.

10:7 REFLECTING ON YOUR JOURNEY AND CELEBRATING SUCCESSES

Imagine standing on a hilltop, looking back at the winding path you've traveled. Each step, whether a stumble or a sprint, has brought you to this moment. Regular reflection on your personal progress is like taking a moment on that hilltop to appreciate the view. It's about acknowledging growth and understanding how far you've come. Keeping a gratitude journal can be a powerful tool in this process. You create a record of achievements and moments of joy by jotting down daily or weekly entries about what you're thankful for. This practice enhances your appreciation for life's small wins. It provides a tangible reminder of your progress when doubts creep in. Setting aside time for self-reflection allows you to pause and consider what you've achieved, what you've learned, and where you want to go next. This quiet moment of introspection can offer clarity and reinforce your purpose.

Celebrating big and small successes can significantly boost your motivation and morale. Recognizing milestones, whether finishing a challenging project or simply sticking to a new habit for a month, validates your efforts and fuels your drive. Planning rewards or celebrations for these accomplishments can enhance this effect. These celebrations need not be grandiose; sometimes, a simple treat or a day off can be enough. The key is to acknowledge the effort you've put in and the progress you've made. This recognition not only enhances your motivation but also builds your confidence, encouraging you to tackle new challenges with renewed enthusiasm.

Maintaining momentum and motivation is crucial to sustaining progress. Revisiting your goals regularly can help you stay focused and aligned with your aspirations. Goals may evolve, and that's perfectly okay. Being open to revising them as you grow ensures they remain relevant and inspiring. Seeking inspiration from role models or mentors is another effective strategy. Their stories and insights can provide fresh perspectives and ignite your passion. Engaging with those who have walked similar paths can offer encouragement and remind you of what's possible. Their experiences can act as guiding lights, illuminating the way forward.

Sharing your successes with others can also be profoundly rewarding. When you share your achievements, you celebrate your progress and inspire those around you. Whether telling your story within community groups or celebrating with friends and family, these shared moments create connections and foster a sense of community. They remind you that you're part of something bigger than yourself, and your successes contribute to the collective joy and inspiration of others. This communal celebration can strengthen bonds and create a supportive network that uplifts everyone involved.

CONCLUSION

"Success is the sum of small efforts, repeated day in and day out."

— ROBERT COLLIER

As you end this journey, let's revisit the essential life skills and strategies we've explored together. From the initial steps of moving out and managing independent living to mastering culinary skills and home management, you've learned how to navigate the complexities of adult life. We delved into financial literacy, equipping you with tools for budgeting, understanding credit, and investing in your future. Your health and wellbeing were prioritized with practical advice on insurance, preventative care, mindfulness, and a balanced lifestyle.

In professional development, you gained insights on crafting standout resumes, acing interviews, and building professional networks. Your relationships, both personal and professional, were nurtured through effective communication, conflict resolution, and setting healthy boundaries. We also explored digital literacy and online safety, ensuring you're prepared in today's interconnected world. Social etiquette and cultural competence were highlighted to help you navigate diverse environments gracefully. Personal safety and preparedness were emphasized, giving you the confidence to handle emergencies. Finally, we focused on personal growth and life planning, encouraging you to set goals and embrace a growth mindset.

Key takeaways include the importance of budgeting and financial discipline, laying the foundation for independence. Maintaining a healthy lifestyle through regular exercise, balanced nutrition, and adequate sleep empowers you to tackle daily challenges. Practical communication skills enhance your relationships and professional interactions. Mastering job-related skills opens doors to career success. Embracing a growth mindset enables you to adapt and thrive amidst life's hurdles.

Now, reflect on your journey. Think about how much you've grown since you first felt the weight of adult responsibilities. The skills and strategies you've gained have transformed you. You are no longer overwhelmed but prepared and confident to face what lies ahead.

As you progress, I encourage you to apply what you have learned. Start by choosing one or two skills or strategies to implement daily. Consider creating a budget or practicing mindfulness exercises. These small steps lead to significant changes, building your confidence and independence over time.

Remember, adulthood is an ongoing journey of learning and self-improvement. Seek out additional resources, mentors, and communities that can support your growth. Never stop learning, exploring, and improving. This mindset will keep you resilient and adaptable as you navigate the complexities of life.

You are capable of achieving success and fulfillment. As you continue your journey, let this powerful quote guide you: "The future belongs to those who believe in the beauty of their dreams." Your dreams are within reach, and you have the skills and determination to make them a reality.

Thank you for investing your time and effort into this book. Your courage and determination to take steps toward becoming a successful, confident, and independent adult are commendable. It has been a privilege to accompany you on this journey.

I invite you to share your experiences and insights from the book. Engage with online communities or social media platforms related to our themes for further discussion and support. Your journey doesn't end here, and I am excited to see where it takes you next.

REFERENCES

How to Decide Where to Live | Real Estate | U.S. News https://realestate.usnews.com/real-estate/articles/how-to-decide-where-to-live

How to Find a Roommate: A Complete Guide https://www.common.com/blog/2021/09/how-to-find-a-roommate/

Residential Tenants' Rights Guide https://ag.ny.gov/sites/default/files/tenants_rights.pdf

What Is Renters Insurance and What Does It Cover? https://www.allstate.com/resources/renters-insurance/what-does-renters-insurance-cover

80+ Budget Friendly Meal Prep Ideas https://www.budgetbytes.com/category/extra-bytes/budget-friendly-meal-prep/

8 Smart Shopping Tips to Save on Groceries https://nutrail.com/blogs/nutrail-blog/8-smart-strategies-to-save-money-on-groceries?srsltid=AfmBOoosiiWbJKsOnFlxFbuLXlODluWsLtWMfElPWaKX72G8BG5YofNs

10 Essential Kitchen Tools for Beginner Cooks - Bon Appetit https://www.bonappetit.com/story/10-essential-kitchen-tools-beginner-cooks?srsltid=AfmBOoptyd4kgwgTBVHFLqI5jkfk-vMjvEdEYbhIltbZ65Nh-SO5oiVO

17 Laundry Room Organizing Tips to Simplify Wash Day https://www.marthastewart.com/274358/laundry-room-organizing-ideas

How to Write a Resume That Stands Out https://hbr.org/2022/05/how-to-write-a-resume-that-will-stand-out

Common Interview Questions and How To Answer Them https://www.indeed.com/career-advice/interviewing/top-interview-questions-and-answers

Professional Etiquette https://futurestitch.com/pages/professional-etiquette

How to Build A Professional Network on LinkedIn https://www.linkedin.com/pulse/how-build-professional-network-linkedin-marie-ennis-o-connor

The Best Budget Apps for 2025 https://www.nerdwallet.com/article/finance/best-budget-apps

Understanding Your Credit | Consumer Advice https://consumer.ftc.gov/articles/understanding-your-credit

How To Avoid Credit Card Debt https://www.cnbc.com/select/how-to-avoid-credit-card-debt/

Roth vs. Traditional IRA: Which Is Better for You? https://www.investopedia.com/retirement/roth-vs-traditional-ira-which-is-right-for-you/

HMO vs PPO: Things To Consider - CareFirst https://individual.carefirst.com/individuals-families/health-insurance-basics/how-health-insurance-works/hmo-vs-ppo.page

How to Manage Stress with Mindfulness and Meditation https://www.mindful.org/how-to-manage-stress-with-mindfulness-and-meditation/

Mental Health and Sleep https://www.sleepfoundation.org/mental-health

Fitness program: 5 steps to get started - Mayo Clinic https://www.mayoclinic.org/healthy-lifestyle/fitness/in-depth/fitness/art-20048269

7 Active Listening Techniques For Better Communication https://www.verywellmind.com/what-is-active-listening-3024343

Assertive Communication: Definition, Examples, & ... https://www.berkeleywellbeing.com/assertive-communication.html

The Power of Emotional Intelligence in Relationships https://care-clinics.com/the-power-of-emotional-intelligence-in-relationships/

A Guide to Setting Better Boundaries https://hbr.org/2022/04/a-guide-to-setting-better-boundaries

Why we need etiquette - Whitman Wire https://whitmanwire.com/opinion/2023/04/06/why-we-need-etiquette

How Cultural Competence Improves Communication https://degree.astate.edu/online-programs/business/masters-strategic-communications/global/cultural-competence-aids-in-communication/

6 Tips for Hosting a Successful Potluck - Savory Online https://www.savoryonline.com/articles/potluck-hosting-tips/

World Travelers of America: Worldwide Tipping Guide https://worldtravelers.org/travel-tips-tipping-guide.asp

Microsoft Digital Defense Report 2023 (MDDR) https://www.microsoft.com/en-us/security/security-insider/microsoft-digital-defense-report-2023

The Importance of Etiquette in Digital Communication https://www.skillmaker.edu.au/the-importance-of-etiquette-in-digital-communication

How to Protect and Reduce Your Digital Footprint https://www.statefarm.com/simple-insights/family/how-to-reduce-and-protect-your-digital-footprint

Essential Networking Strategies for Young Professionals to ... https://www.socialmediabutterflyblog.com/2024/04/essential-networking-strategies-for-young-professionals-to-build-lasting-career-connections/

First Aid Steps | Perform First Aid https://www.redcross.org/take-a-class/first-aid/performing-first-aid/first-aid-steps?srsltid=AfmBOopecQPNBbEqcImbayr_UC37GmoJ63fiThKrKg7oBzlkDtsrGEP

Make A Plan https://www.ready.gov/plan

Fire Safety Equipment List: Protecting Lives And Property https://inspecttrack.com/fire-equipment-inspection/fire-safety-equipment/

Travel & Safety Tips to Know Before You Go - Global PSU https://global.psu.edu/article/travel-safety-tips-know-you-go/

How To Write SMART Goals in 5 Steps (With Examples) https://www.indeed.com/career-advice/career-development/how-to-write-smart-goals

Carol Dweck: A Summary of Growth and Fixed Mindsets https://fs.blog/carol-dweck-mindset/

Coping with Change: Strategies for Managing Stress and ... https://serenehealth.com/coping-with-change-strategies-for-managing-stress-and-embracing-personal-growth-during-life-transitions/

Developing Your Support System - UB School of Social Work https://socialwork.buffalo.edu/resources/self-care-starter-kit/additional-self-care-resources/developing-your-support-system.html

Printed in Dunstable, United Kingdom